YOUR
THREE SECOND
WINDOW

Changing Everyday Moments
into
Extraordinary Opportunities for Success

By

Darby Roach

Editor: Barbara Azzato

New York

Your Three Second Window

Changing Every Day Moments Into Extraordinary Opportunities For Success

ISBN 978-1-60037-713-6

Library of Congress Control Number:

MORGAN · JAMES
THE ENTREPRENEURIAL PUBLISHER

Morgan James Publishing, LLC
1225 Franklin Ave., STE 325
Garden City, NY 11530-1693
Toll Free 800-485-4943
www.MorganJamesPublishing.com

In an effort to support local communities, raise awareness and funds, Morgan James Publishing donates one percent of all book sales for the life of each book to Habitat for Humanity. Get involved today, visit **www.HelpHabitatForHumanity.org**.

For Brittney, Annie and Maren

Also by Darby Roach

Think Fast

Snoqualmie Pass

Steep

Contents

What Is Your Three Second Window? 1

Introduction to Your Three Second Window 3

Part One: Successful You

Chapter 1   Your Three Second Window 7

Chapter 2   The Beauty of Success 33

Chapter 3   The Myth of the Logical Decision 59

Part Two: Your Environment for Success

Chapter 4   Designing for Success 83

Chapter 5   Impulse Nation 109

Chapter 6   Why We Buy 125

Part Three: The Business of Success

Chapter 7   Strategy for Success 145

Chapter 8   The Power of Three 171

Chapter 9   Picasso's Napkin 191

Summary: Your Successful Life

Chapter 10 The Holistic Effect 223

About the Author 229

Chapter End Notes 231

What Is Your Three Second Window?

Your Three Second Window is the moment when you make a choice. It's that brief flash of time when you decide whether you like someone, something, someplace, or you don't. How you feel about things and people determines how you will act. If you like a person, place or thing, your act will likely be a positive one. The act might be small, such as deciding in favor of one flavor of ice cream over another. Or the act might carry more consequences, such as deciding which city to live in or whom to marry.

Your life is filled with Three Second Windows. You have dozens, even hundreds, of them every day. Each Three Second Window is vibrating with energy, alive with potential and ripe with chance; a portal from which many possible trajectories emerge. It's the intersection of preparation and opportunity, that moment when the baseball meets the bat. It's unique to you and to your time and place. It's the chance you get to change everyday moments into extraordinary opportunities for success.

The trick to taking advantage of Your Three Second Windows is learning to recognize them, to understand how your subconscious brain processes information and communicates it to your consciousness through feelings, and to use your own instincts to make the kinds of decisions that lead to success.

In *Your Three Second Window*, you'll get to look at the latest research in brain physiology and chemistry and see how you can take control of your own subconscious—and influence those of others—to bring harmony to your life and achieve successful personal and career relationships. You'll learn how to use the connections between aesthetics and the pleasure and decision-making centers of the brain to become more successful in everything you do.

Introduction to Your Three Second Window

This book is about using the connections between aesthetics and the pleasure and decision-making centers of the brain to be more successful in everything you do. We all are more or less aware of them, and I've discovered in my more than thirty years of teaching and practicing my profession, that artists and designers seem to be more aware of those connections than non-artists. This observation has led me to one inescapable conclusion: Artists and designers see the world differently than others do. I could never put my finger on exactly what it was that gave creative people this different perspective, but I knew it had something to do with the way they were able to tap into their own intuition and emotions. I have always wondered how artists and designers know how to make things that other people like. Over the years, I've asked myself and other artists and designers this same question: "How do you know when you've got it right?" The answer has always been, after a bit of head scratching, "Well... it just *feels* right!"

I never found that answer to be completely satisfying. But nevertheless, I incorporated the idea into my teaching and practice. The first thing I taught my beginning students was how to get in touch with their intuition, their subconscious. You see, I knew the aesthetic experience dwelt not in thinking—not in the conscious mind—but in the gut, the subconscious. I understood that to be able to make things that appeal to others, the artist has to elevate the subconscious mechanism that controls the aesthetic experience to the level of consciousness. The difference between artists and designers and everyone else is the ability to consciously influence their own and others' subconscious minds. Artists and designers are able to consciously exploit the connections between the world of form: aesthetics—and the realm of the subconscious: the pleasure and decision-making centers of the brain.

I strove to instill this basic skill in my students, and those who were particularly adept at it, I noticed, were the most successful artists and designers. But there was something else about those students that set them apart from their less skillful classmates. It seemed they were more confident, more popular and better liked, and they enjoyed more successful careers after graduation. This observation got me thinking. *Maybe there's more to this than just being a good artist or designer.*

There was some mysterious and indefinable quality about those students that made them successful not just as artists and designers, but as people. They seemed to enjoy life in all its spheres. What was going on? About this time, neuroscience and new brain imaging technology were being developed and used to map the aesthetic experience. I began to read and research and discovered something amazing in its simplicity. *We like the people, places and things we like because they make us feel good!*

Now for the first time in human experience, we are able to understand how and why we like the things we like. We know what parts of the brain are responsible for producing and releasing certain chemicals that give us that delicious feeling that our human needs are being met. And better than that, we can use that knowledge in practical, everyday situations to create success in all spheres of our lives—social, environmental and professional.

In this book, you'll learn how the brain processes information to generate that good feeling we get when we see something we like—and how to use it to your own benefit. You'll learn easy techniques for exploiting the connections between aesthetics and the pleasure and decision-making centers of the brain to quickly establish strong, positive relationships with others, develop a home and work environment that invites success, and have a more satisfying and successful career.

Through simple exercises that build on each other, you'll learn how to tap into your intuition and emotions and use them to change your everyday moments into extraordinary opportunities for success. You'll become a master of Your Three Second Window.

How to Use This Book

This book is divided into three parts. Each part introduces concepts and provides exercises designed to teach you how to tap into your own intuition and emotions and project them in powerful and beneficial ways every day.

Part One: *You'll learn how to quickly create positive connections with other people.* Most communication happens subconsciously. The key is understanding how the brain's structures, systems and chemicals work to produce the great feeling that occurs when our human needs are being met. You'll learn the basic principles that govern the connections between aesthetics and the pleasure and decision-making centers of the brain.

Part Two: *You'll learn how to create home and work environments that invite success.* Understanding how things get designed and manufactured and how space affects mood helps you shape a home and a workplace that bring joy, nurture the soul and set the stage for success.

Part Three: *You'll learn how to create a more fulfilling and successful career.* Visual communication is more vital than ever to getting ahead in the business world. I'll share strategies and tactics learned from my twenty-five years of professional design and communication practice and teaching to give you the power to create like a pro, too.

Part One: Successful You

Chapter 1

Your Three Second Window

Perhaps the most important and powerful Three Second Windows in your life have to do with personal relationships—professional, plutonic and romantic. They're also the easiest to recognize and understand because they stand out so unambiguously. When you meet someone for the first time, you know instantly and without doubt whether you're going to like him or her. The brain mechanisms and chemicals are working at their most basic level when it comes to the like or dislike of others. A lot of study has been done in the area of neuroscience and personal relationships, and it's from these studies that much of the information about other kinds of Three Second Windows grows. That's why the discussion of how and why you like other people is the best place to start our exploration of the many facets of Your Three Second Window.

You Are a Force of Nature

You've experienced it: that delicious feeling that comes over you when you spot an attractive stranger for the first time. Maybe you're at a party or a business function. It could be at the supermarket or even in an elevator. If you're lucky, you get to chat a while, and chances are that brief conversation will validate and increase your original feelings of attraction. The other person will send all the right signals, meet your gaze, exude confidence, share your sense of humor, have similar interests, use some of the same slang. It's one of those Three Second Windows that happen frequently in your life and sometimes lead to great things.

Afterward, you'll find your thoughts wandering. You'll imagine future encounters and begin planning ways to arrange the next meeting. You'll tell your friends and fuss in front of the mirror a little more than usual. In a day or two, you'll begin to feel a sense of longing, perhaps a twinge of bittersweet melancholy; you sure do wish you could get together again.

The good news is, he or she is probably having the same feelings about you.

It's love at first sight. Neuroscientists call it instant attraction—a genuine Three Second Window, and it's the real thing, biological in nature. You see, our subconscious brains have evolved to be able to spot a likely mate, one genetically fit to spread our genes around, and it's important to understand how and why instant attraction works as a function of brain activity, evolution and biology and as a driving force of nature in all aspects of our lives. In this chapter, we'll visit with Jessie, who not too long ago had a Three Second Window and fell in love at first sight with a man she met at a business dinner. We'll look at how her subconscious brain was able to pick up on certain physical cues to single out the right guy from a crowd and inform her of its choice through the production of a neurochemical that created a delicious feeling.

Jessie's in Love

"It was his eyes," Jessie says, "that made me fall in love." Jessie (not her real name) is in her early forties, has an advanced degree and runs her own successful business. She's a no-nonsense woman. She's a nice person, too, the kind who will juggle her schedule at the last minute just to meet you for coffee. But don't let her generous side give you the wrong impression. Jessie's known for being able to hold her own against high-powered businessmen every day. Her friends will tell you she's not one to be easily fooled or swept off her feet.

"I can't explain what happened," she tells me, shaking her head and smiling wryly when I ask how she met and fell in love with her boyfriend. Jessie is sitting across the table from me at Starbucks, and she wraps her hands around the cup, running a thumb across the porcelain before continuing. "When he walked into the room, I got one look at him and I was sold."

Jessie says there's no logical explanation for the way she felt that night. "We were at a business function, you know, one of those rubber chicken dinners where a bunch of us in the same industry gather to schmooze and trade gossip. I was chatting with a friend when a stranger walked in the door. He caught my eye right away. I can't put my finger on what attracted me to him. I guess it was the crazy feeling I got. It was a little thrill that went up my spine and made my scalp tingle." Jessie was experiencing a Three Second Window that would be the beginning of a beautiful relationship the stuff of romantic songs, novels and movies—love at first sight or, as a neuroscientist would say, instant attraction.

But was she? Does love at first sight actually exist, and who really believes in it?

Some forward-thinking researchers are trying to answer that very question. Earl Naumann, Ph.D. and author of the book *Love at First Sight: The Stories and Science Behind Instant Attraction*, did a study in which he interviewed fifteen hundred men and women. What he found was that most people either believed in it or had actually felt it: Sixty-four percent said they believed in love at first sight, and fifty-eight percent said they had experienced it. Even people who don't believe in it, the study found, are as likely as anyone else to fall in love at first sight.

Jessie is a writer and an art historian with a high appreciation for aesthetics. "Sometimes I think it was just that he was so good looking, but it was more than that. I've seen lots of handsome men, but they never made me feel the way he did. How do you explain love?"

Researchers who study love at first sight believe it involves a set of structures, chemicals and networks in the brain called the reward system and that it's there to help ensure survival. The reward system is the mechanism behind every Three Second Window. You might think of it as having parts similar to the parts of your computer. There are your senses, which can be compared to input devices such as the keyboard and Internet connection. Your brain stem processes input the way your computer's central processing unit does. And your neocortex, your consciousness, is like your computer's screen and speakers: It's where the images are displayed and the sounds are played. When you see another person, the reward system springs into action. Your senses take in information about him or her. Your brain stem processes what your eyes see. Through evolution, we've developed a kind of database or template of things and situations that will give us a survival advantage. Your subconscious brain compares the new information with your template and, if there's a match, bingo. The pieces of the puzzle fall into place, and your reward system produces certain chemicals and sends them to your neocortex. The neocortex is stimulated, and you experience the same rush of good feelings Jessie did the first time she saw her guy. You've fallen in love at first sight!

Good Vibrations

To understand Your Three Second Window and why the modern human brain is able to spot good mates so fast, we need to go back in time to the Pleistocene epoch. The Pleistocene, which started about one and a half million years ago and ended a mere ten thousand years ago, is the period when we became truly human. This stage of human evolution saw a lot of changes in our brains, and by the end of the Pleistocene, we had arrived. People had the same brain structure and capacity and looked about the same as we do today. Through natural selection, we had developed certain hardwired preferences that evolved to ensure our survival as a species.

In his book *The Mating Mind*, evolutionary psychologist Geoffrey Miller proposes an interesting theory about the development of the reward system that makes a lot of sense. As you might guess, it has a lot to do with sex, and it goes like this: Some of our early Pleistocene ancestors were genetically better equipped to survive than others. They survived at a greater rate and had more children, who in turn passed their genes along to their children, who passed them along to *their* children. The result was that, over time, Pleistocene people developed a preference for mates with good genes similar to their own.

According to Miller, they were—as we are today—very attuned subconsciously to what he calls fitness indicators. Fitness indicators are those outward signs people exhibit that cue your reward system to respond positively and release a feel-good drug called dopamine. There will be more about this miraculous chemical later, but for now it's enough to know that dopamine is the brain chemical that makes you feel pleasure and lets you know your human needs are being met. Under the spell of dopamine, you think, *Now, there's someone I really like!*

The Dopamine Test

Pause and think about a person you love: your spouse, a parent or child, a close friend. Picture that person's face. Think about the eyes, the shape of the face, the curve of the chin, the complexion. If you have a photograph handy, study it. Now think of a moment you shared with that person that was especially dear to you. Got it? Now anticipate the next time you will be with that person. How does it make you feel? Do you get a little bounce of euphoria? Is that a smile forming on your lips? If so, your loved one has passed the dopamine test; the thought of him or her has caused your brain to release this marvelous chemical, the feel-good drug your reward system is producing to tell you that you love that person. You're responding to your loved one's fitness indicators through your own Three Second Window. You might even decide to give him or her a call, thinking that the sound of his or her voice will make you feel even better. Such a situation is a classic example of how aesthetics—your attraction to your loved one—and your pleasure and decision-making brain centers work together to influence what you think and how you act.

Our faces are rich with fitness indicators. The eyes, mouth, nose, chin, cheeks and jaw, as well as the skin that covers and surrounds these features, tell us the most about a person's fitness to reproduce. Clear, steady eyes; straight, white teeth; a noble nose; healthy-looking lips; and smooth unblemished skin are all things we find attractive because, through survival of the fittest, our ancestors' reward systems incorporated these features into their templates as indicators of good health and good genes. Our ancestors were heavily influenced by aesthetics and had Three Second Windows in which they chose their mates by the way they made them feel, just as we do today.

There are many fitness indicators, but symmetry stands out as one of the most telling. Symmetry seems to be so important because it is a broad signifier of the absence of genetic weakness. Symmetrical faces and bodies are proof of a person's genetic ability to resist pathogens and diseases that can cause physical unevenness. An example of this principle is represented by the asymmetrical facial appearance of people who have suffered partial paralysis due to hemorrhagic stroke. Among other things, high blood pressure and weakened blood vessels cause these kinds of strokes, and both can be genetic in nature. Through natural selection, the Pleistocene brain became sensitive to the inward meaning of such outward fitness indicators as symmetry until they were permanently embedded in the reward system. In this way, researchers think, symmetry became one of the primary parts of the modern brain's template for choosing a good mate.

Today we still prefer faces that are symmetrical. In a study undertaken by researchers Steven Gangestad and Randy Thornhill[1], photographs of men's and women's faces were measured at precise points to find those that were most symmetrical. These photos were then shown to subjects along with photos of less even faces. Not surprisingly, the most symmetrical faces were perceived as the most attractive.

This study is only one of many investigations into why we fall in love at first sight. Poets, writers and philosophers have pondered the magic and mystery of love at first sight for ages. But until recently, the physiological and psychological causes have been hidden and just as mysterious. Only within the last several years has science been able to seriously tackle the mystery of the Three Second Window and love at first sight.

One of those who has taken on the challenge of demystifying love at first sight is Helen Fisher, Ph.D., of Rutgers University[2]: who, along with researchers at the State University of New York and the Albert Einstein College of Medicine, conducted a study of volunteers who had been in love for less than six months. The subjects were placed in a functional magnetic resonance imaging (fMRI) scanner, the latest in brain scanning technology, and shown photos of their loved ones. The fMRI is a wondrous machine that allows researchers to look inside the living human brain and watch it react to what the eyes see. It works by passing harmless magnetic pulses through brain tissue. Parts of the brain that become more active during stimulation receive increased blood flow, which can be seen in the scans. With the fMRI, Fisher and her colleagues could see different parts of the subjects' brains "light up" with increased blood flow as they viewed photos of their loved ones.

They observed that two parts of the brain were particularly stimulated by the photos: the caudate nucleus and the ventral tegmental area (VTA), both of which are associated with the reward system. The caudate nucleus is an interesting bit of anatomy. It's an important part of the neural network that generates arousal, produces feelings of pleasure and motivates you to pursue rewards. Another part of the reward system, the VTA, is a small structure in the brain stem that is rich in dopamine-producing cells. The drug dopamine is an important product of the reward system. It makes you feel good, and when you experience its effect you want more. Your reward system produces dopamine during Your Three Second Window to create attraction and drive you to pursue the object of your desire. When you think of a loved one, you get a good feeling—a dopamine high.

Fisher observed increased activity in the VTA, suggesting a release of dopamine. She concluded that when subjects viewed photos of their loved ones, the VTA produced a flood of dopamine, which caused the caudate nucleus to become super-activated, resulting in a sense of arousal. Dopamine is a strong drug that has been shown in some studies to produce a reaction similar to the one caused by cocaine. Dopamine can make you giddy, light-headed, even euphoric. It can make your heart beat rapidly, increase your breathing rate and cause you to pour sweat. These are all reactions Jessie says she felt the night she first laid eyes on her guy and gave him the dopamine test. "My mouth was dry and my palms were damp. I actually think my heart skipped a beat!"

It turns out that love really is a drug!

And its strength can be measured, too. Fisher developed a metric to evaluate the intensity of feeling each test subject had toward his or her loved ones before the fMRI scan. Fisher calls it the Passionate Love Scale, or PLS. The PLS is reproduced here so you can use it to measure the intensity you feel toward your partner, too, just for fun.

PLS scoring runs from a low of fifteen, meaning oops!, to a high of one hundred and thirty-five, which indicates you are head over heels. Fisher found a direct correlation between the level of intensity as determined by the PLS, the amount of dopamine released and the resulting rush that test subjects felt. What this means is that some of us have more active reward systems and are able to experience a more intense arousal. It comes as no surprise that some people are more easily aroused than others and that the degree of emotion can increase or decrease with time.

The Passionate Love Scale

These items ask you to describe how you feel when you are passionately in love. Think of the person whom you love most passionately right now. If you are not in love right now, think of the last person you loved passionately. If you have never been in love, think of the person whom you came closest to caring for in that way. Choose your answer remembering how you felt at the time when your feelings were the most intense.

1. I would feel deep despair if_____left me.

2. Sometimes I feel I can't control my thoughts: they are obsessively on_____.

3. I feel happy when I am doing something to make_____happy.

4. I would rather be with_____than anyone else.

5. I'd get jealous if I thought_____were falling in love with someone else.

6. I yearn to know more about_____.

7. I want_____physically, emotionally, mentally.

8. I have an endless appetite for affection from_____.

9. For me,_____is the perfect romantic partner.

10. I sense my body responding when_____touches me.

11. _____always seems to be on my mind.

12. I want_____to know me—my thoughts, my fears, and my hopes.

13. I eagerly look for signs indicating_____'s desire for me.

14. I possess a powerful attraction for_____.

15. I get very depressed when things don't go right in my relationship with_____.

Not at all   Moderately   Definitely

1 2 3 4 5 6 7 8 9

1 2 3 4 5 6 7 8 9

1 2 3 4 5 6 7 8 9

1 2 3 4 5 6 7 8 9

1 2 3 4 5 6 7 8 9

1 2 3 4 5 6 7 8 9

1 2 3 4 5 6 7 8 9

1 2 3 4 5 6 7 8 9

1 2 3 4 5 6 7 8 9

1 2 3 4 5 6 7 8 9

1 2 3 4 5 6 7 8 9

1 2 3 4 5 6 7 8 9

1 2 3 4 5 6 7 8 9

1 2 3 4 5 6 7 8 9

1 2 3 4 5 6 7 8 9

Another metric used in Fisher's study was the Affect Intensity Measure, or AIM. The AIM is a series of yes or no questions that rate an individual's general tendency to experience emotions. "I get overly enthusiastic" and "Sad movies touch me deeply" are examples. At the end of the study, researchers compared PLS and AIM scores to see whether very emotional people were more likely to experience love at first sight. The result? Less emotional people were just as likely to experience love at first sight as people self-described as highly emotional. It turns out we're all equally susceptible to the love bug.

Like Forces Attract

It's interesting and useful to hear what other people think about love at first sight and to understand the mechanics of it, but it's perhaps even more valuable to get a handle on the kinds of stimuli that cause your reward system to work the way it does to create Your Three Second Windows. Just what is it that makes you go gaga over another person? What is it about some people that make them attractive? What does it take to pass the dopamine test?

It's said you can't choose your family. But oddly enough, in a way, you do. Think about your significant other. Chances are, you share some physical similarities. His or her face might have the same general shape, or you both may have similar height/weight proportions. There were, no doubt, a lot of factors that drew you together, but whether you consciously took it into account, having a familiar appearance similar to your own was probably one of them. Your parents responded to the same fitness indicators when they chose to be together, too. When you look at your mother or father, your brother or sister, you no doubt will see a family resemblance. You might have your mother's nose and your father's eyes, you might have the same color hair as your brother or sister. In turn, *your* offspring will carry on some of your and your mate's genes, too, and reveal them through their outward appearances—their fitness indicators—as well.

Researchers at the Virtual Human Interaction Lab at Stanford University were curious to learn just how strong an attractor similar looks really are. To find out, they conducted a study just two weeks before the 2004 presidential election that involved morphing photos of John Kerry and George W. Bush with photos of volunteers[3]. One-third of the study participants were shown unretouched photos, one-third were shown photos of Kerry and Bush morphed with those of strangers and one-third saw photos of Kerry and Bush that had been combined with pictures of their own faces. The volunteers in this last group were unable to consciously recognize their own facial characteristics when subtly combined with the photos of the candidates. Not surprisingly, the study results showed that subjects were more likely to vote for the candidate who looked like them than the candidate who did not. This study contributed to the already voluminous data that suggest we do find people who look like ourselves more attractive. In Jessie's case, her experience seems to bear out this theory of the attraction of similarity. Jessie is a runner and enjoys the outdoors. It turned out that her guy is a runner, too, and an outdoorsman. Did Jessie's reward system spot his runner's physique and his suntanned complexion and like what it saw?

Like forces attract. In Jessie's case, the initial attraction was instant and based solely on looks. Her experience supports the idea that people with similar physical characteristics tend to find each other attractive. When you are in social or business situations that call for interpersonal interaction, you of course want the other person to like you too, to be drawn to you. And if you share similar looks, then that's going to happen more easily. But how do you establish rapport with people who are dissimilar in appearance to yourself? How do you make others' Three Second Windows work to your advantage? How do you pass the dopamine test? The answer lies in the fact that what really draws people together is attractiveness—in all its forms. The most obvious form of attractiveness is physical appearance, but there are other ways to create immediate empathy and attraction, too. Jessie, on reflection, allows that her guy's looks influenced the way she felt; still, she insists it was mostly his eyes that got to her. "He looked right into my eyes, he seemed so confident."

Who hasn't felt that little thrill, the allure of a sultry gaze? When someone says it's chemistry, they aren't kidding, and there's even science to back it up. Malia Mason, who, when she was a student at the psychology department at Dartmouth, researched the effect that eyes have on perceived attractiveness[4]. Mason writes that "we do know that gaze is a very potent attentional cue. In fact, there's evidence that when someone looks at us, it's psychologically arousing, and there are these brain regions that get more engaged." Mason bases her conclusion on the research of others, as well as on a study she conducted in which subjects were asked to view a series of pictures of faces. Through computer manipulation, the images were made to look toward or away from the viewer. Both men and women said they found the people who seemed to look away less likeable than those who seemed to meet their gaze.

Poets muse that the eyes are the windows to the soul. When you meet another's gaze, you send a message more succinct than any words can convey. You open yourself up and invite the other person in. It's an act of honesty and intimacy. What could be more attractive?

Meaningful eye contact isn't a skill we learn later in life and use solely as a tool of seduction. It's the most natural of human traits and something we're born with. The infant, just becoming self-aware, practices it, is enthralled by the gaze of another, revealing a kind of early confidence born of innocence. Even adolescents, those at perhaps the most self-conscious age, seem to instinctively derive pleasure from a prolonged gaze.

Scientists at the Institute for Human Behaviour Research in Andechs, Germany, were interested in finding out just how strong a role eye contact plays in the teenage mating ritual. They conducted a study involving a group of high school students from fifty different schools and invited them to a lecture where selected pairs—a boy from one school and a girl from another—were separated from the group and left alone in a room, ostensibly to view videos. After ten minutes, the students, who were secretly filmed, were asked a series of questions such as "Would you go to a cinema with this person?" and "So, do you think he or she would go with you?" The students' responses were later compared with what the researchers observed on the secret film.

What researchers discovered supports the idea that the eyes and eye contact have a powerful ability to activate our reward systems and create positive Three Second Windows. Researchers reported that the students who liked each other gave a lot of signals indicating mutual attraction. One of the strongest and most common signals was eye contact.

Jessie says, "He looked right into my eyes. You have to be pretty sure of yourself to do that with someone you just met. I got the feeling right away that here was someone who had nothing to hide. Someone I could trust."

It's nothing short of miraculous that confidence, honesty and an invitation to intimacy can be conveyed with a single glance, yet it's common and universal, a sure sign that nature has provided us with a very powerful way to create and signal attraction to another human being. When you meet someone for the first time, the most important part of your interaction that you have control over will be appropriate eye contact. That first meeting, that initial Three Second Window, will determine the course of the relationship from that moment on. That's why it's so important to be aware of the opportunity to create rapport with that person through the eyes. I've had people ask me, "But what is appropriate eye contact?" There's no one answer to that question, because it depends upon the individual. I believe we instinctively know how long and how often to meet the other person's gaze. Too long can become uncomfortable, too brief seems shifty. Generally, I've found the best way to gauge 'appropriateness' is to observe the other person's eyes. They will let you know what is appropriate. Usually a few seconds seems about right. Watch his or her eyes and mentally time how long he or she holds your gaze before looking off and then returning. Use that interval he or she find comfortable to gauge what is appropriate.

Appropriate eye contact varies from person to person and setting to setting. In a busy café, the hustle and bustle will naturally draw the eyes away more often, and that's okay; it shows you have an interest in the world around you. In a quiet, candlelit bistro, however, eye contact will usually be longer and more meaningful. You're saying, "You're the most important person in the world to me." Your eyes are the most expressive part of your body. Use them to create Three Second Windows that work to your advantage. Use eye contact to emphasize important points in the conversation, to indicate interest, surprise, or delight at what the other person is saying. Don't be afraid to hold eye contact a fraction of a second longer than what is comfortable to dramatize a moment—just don't do it too often.

Using expressive eye contact to create rapport with others is the most natural thing in the world. Babies do it. It's only after we've erroneously learned to hide our emotions that we tend to play down eye contact.

Making meaningful eye contact doesn't mean you need to take acting lessons or be disingenuous; on the contrary, it simply requires being yourself and letting that show through your eyes. Remember, you're communicating in the most powerful way possible. Your eyes give you the greatest advantage to make every Three Second Window an extraordinary opportunity for success. Learn to recognize these opportunities and don't let a single one pass you by. Follow these simple tips about eye contact and you'll be well on your way to passing the dopamine test with flying colors.

Of course, physical similarities and the eyes aren't the only things that attract us to others, and there seems to be some variance between what the sexes find most alluring. Naumann's study on perception of love at first sight, cited earlier in this chapter, reported a slight difference in what women and men found attractive. Women more often identified kindness, humor, fun and self-confidence as desirable personality traits in men. Men, on the other hand, identified being fun, outgoing and communicative as desirable traits in women. But both men and women ranked attractiveness as the number-one desirable physical attribute. Biology is destiny.

But what does it mean to say someone is attractive? Attractive can be a pretty fuzzy word. It can mean a lot of different things to a lot of people. That said, both men and women in Naumann's study often agreed that the eyes are a powerfully attractive physical trait and that fun is a highly desirable character trait. Is there a connection between the two? Is there something in our subconscious that can determine in an instant whether a person is fun, kind, caring, outgoing or confident just by looking in his or her eyes?

X-Factors and Your Three Second Window

Some people just seem to be naturally attractive. They have a powerful presence and draw attention wherever they go. They make the most out of each and every Three Second Window. They rarely flunk the dopamine test. But their appeal goes beyond their looks; in fact, it almost seems that their attractive appearances are created by their personalities. They have that certain indescribable something that makes us want to be around them. A few of them have parlayed their natural attraction into world-famous reputations and for good reason: They are masterful at the art of their Three Second Windows.

Beverly Palmer, professor of psychology at the California State University at Dominguez Hills, tells of a meeting she had with President Bill Clinton. "He was speaking here in L.A., and I had an opportunity to meet him," she says. "He makes immediate eye contact and sustains it correctly while he is listening. The result? He's actually one hundred percent more charismatic than he comes across in any kind of media. You feel like you're the most important thing to him at that particular moment."

Why are people like Bill Clinton so adept at stimulating our reward systems and turning each moment into an extraordinary opportunity for success? Is it a learned talent or an instinct? According to an article in *Psychology Today*, it's a little of both. Carlin Flora writes that several personality traits make people able to draw others to them instantly with a force similar to gravity[5]. Some of us are born with one or more of these traits, while others nurture or develop them later in life. Flora calls them the X-factors and says such prominent cultural icons as Oprah Winfrey, Nelson Mandela and Bill Clinton possess them. According to Flora, the X-factors are charisma, chutzpah, joie de vivre and grace.

Charisma

A key ingredient of charisma, Flora says, is synchrony—the ability to "sync" with others—and some people seem to be naturally good at it. It's something we're born with, but some people are able to cultivate it and put it to greater use than others. People who have this trait unconsciously adjust to others in speech, posture and other verbal and nonverbal ways. About charisma, Flora quotes White House reporter Helen Thomas. "Kennedy had it…he was inspiring and magnetic. He gave us hope. [He] radiated that onward-and-upward good feeling." Synchrony, then, is the ability to stimulate our reward systems by seeming to be like us and to more closely match our genetic makeup.

Chutzpah

"Chutzpah," writes Flora, "makes our jaws drop because it openly challenges our conformist tendencies. It is a behavior that crosses a social norm, not merely to get away with something, but rather to purposefully challenge convention." She gives the example of Erin Brockovich, the legal secretary who helped sue Pacific Gas and Electric Company for a bundle in the mid-1990s, as someone with chutzpah. Her story is an inspiring one, exhibiting courage and determination, very attractive qualities indeed.

Erin Brockovich was working in a California law firm when, while filing legal documents relating to a pro bono case, some medical records caught her eye. With the permission of one of the firm's partners, Brockovich took it on herself to pursue the leads. Conducting investigations that went way beyond her duties (and, some at the time insisted, beyond her capabilities) as secretary, she discovered that the residents of the small town of Hinkley suffered an unusually high level of health problems resulting from exposure to a toxic chemical that was being released into the groundwater by a nearby natural gas compressor station. Brockovich's dogged determination and disregard for the boundaries of behavior considered acceptable for her social and professional position led to the biggest toxic tort injury settlement in U.S. history: three hundred and thirty million dollars. Now that's chutzpah.

People with chutzpah turn their Three Second Windows to their own advantage by taking a dim view of the boundaries placed on them by society. They're the risk takers of the world, the people who have the confidence to roll the dice and put themselves out there. Perhaps it's their boldness, certainly a form of confidence, that stimulates our reward systems.

Joie de Vivre

"People with joie de vivre," Flora says, "are like wind-up dolls that never run down. They are passionate explorers who view their work as play." Another definition is offered by University of Maryland psychologist Nathan Fox. Fox calls it "passionate exuberance" and claims it's something we're born with. In his study of temperament in infants, about ten percent of his subjects possessed this quality. "Positive rewards like social interaction do more for them than they do for others," Fox explains, and he suspects these infants' reward systems function differently. When we observe joie de vivre in another, it might stimulate our reward systems by indicating that the person exhibiting this trait has the energy and drive to be a good provider and suitable mate.

Grace

Grace, Flora says, "is too elusive to pin down in a lab [but] we can catch glimpses of it in studies of characteristics like wisdom and benevolence." Grace is the quality that allows some people to see more and further than the rest. Equanimity, tolerance and wisdom are all traits of grace. Flora offers Nelson Mandela as an example of someone with a great deal of grace. His twenty-seven years in prison gave him perspective, insight and resolve and only added to his stature as a person with grace. It could be that grace activates our reward systems because it is a sign of intelligence—which surely is a survival advantage—and an indicator of exceptionally fit genes.

Exercising Your Own X-Factors

You have the capacity to turn every Three Second Window into an opportunity for success by exercising and developing your own X-factors. Charisma, chutzpah, joie de vivre and grace are all things that you are born with or are capable of developing. It simply comes down to finding those qualities within yourself and expressing them in your own unique way. You probably already have most of the X-factors and use them all the time. Some of us are stronger in one or more factors than in others, so it's important to focus on those that are strong and make them stronger and to honestly evaluate what factors could use a little work. I've put together a short, informal survey based on my past experience that I think will help you see where you are strongest and where you can improve.

Give yourself five points for each yes answer. A score of fifteen or above indicates you probably are pretty strong in that factor. A score below fifteen might mean you need to focus on that particular one.

Charisma
1. Do you genuinely find other people interesting? Yes No
2. When in conversation, do you listen attentively? Yes No
3. Do you respond visibly to other's happiness and sadness? Yes No
4. Do you refrain from talking over others in conversation? Yes No
5. Do you remember what others have said ten minutes after the end of a conversation? Yes No

Chutzpah
1. Have you ever gone skinny dipping? Yes No
2. Do you ever jaywalk? Yes No
3. Have you ever looked at a work of art and thought 'I can do that!" Yes No
4. Have you ever started to write a book? Yes No
5. Have you ever engaged in "risk sports"? Yes No

Joie de Vivre
1. Do you laugh easily? Yes No
2. Are you physically active? Yes No
3. Do you delight in making others laugh? Yes No
4. Have you ever sung in public? Yes No
5. Are you the one who is always planning activities? Yes No

Grace
1. Are you comfortable admitting when you are wrong? Yes No
2. Have you ever given help to a homeless person? Yes No
3. Do your friends come to you for advice? Yes No
4. Do you compromise even when you believe you are right? Yes No
5. Are you the one to solve the disputes of others? Yes No

Jessie's Three Second Window Plan

Your reward system helps you determine which person would make a good mate and motivates you to pursue him or her. The morning after Jessie first met her guy, she was still a bit giddy from the experience. "I started thinking about ways to get back together with him," she says. "I had his e-mail address and I spent the whole day planning how I would arrange another meeting." The good feeling Jessie had experienced was something she wanted to feel again. It's how Your Three Second Window and the reward system work. The rush we get from dopamine drives us to pursue the object of our desire. We want to have that wonderful feeling again, and we feel sad or blue when we're not in its throes. We become, in a way, addicted to the people who trigger our reward systems. Once we experience love at first sight, our conscious brains, or neocortices, begin to plan ways to repeat the feeling.

"After a few days of e-mailing back and forth, we finally met up at a coffee shop." Jessie smiles when she thinks of this second encounter. "The anticipation was absolutely delicious, and when I sat there across the table from him I just felt…I don't know…great! Before we parted that day, we'd already made plans to get together again."

While we all know the power of attraction when we feel it, few of us could give a textbook definition. That's because it has so many different manifestations and can be caused by so many different things. Is it the eyes? Is it a similarity of looks? Is it a combination of many factors or just that one cue that says this person is for me? Can such quick, subconscious decisions be trusted? We're taught that quick decisions are bad decisions—especially when choosing a mate. But does this old saw hold up to scientific investigation? In Naumann's study, over half of the subjects who fell in love at first sight wound up marrying. And these marriages were pretty stable. Seventy-five percent of those who married as a result of love at first sight stayed married. That's a lot better than the U.S. national average—and a real endorsement for making the most of Your Three Second Windows.

When I interviewed Jessie a year after she fell in love at first sight, she and the object of her affection were still going strong. They'd had a few rocky stretches but their relationship after fourteen months had grown richer and more stable. They'd developed new and deeper attachments and had become closer. But the whole thing had started in that Three Second Window when Jessie's reward system produced a quick burst of dopamine and a feeling that this was the man for her. Would she make the same decision again? "I definitely would," she says. "I think my instincts were right."

One on One

As interesting as Jessie's experience is, it's one of those occurrences that doesn't happen very often and by its nature is unplanned and serendipitous. We don't plan to fall in love, nor can we consciously control whom we fall in love with. If it tells us nothing else, all we've learned about how the brain works tells us this much for sure. Yet, there are intentional, practical, *physical* things you can do with your body in all your interpersonal interactions that change them from everyday moments into extraordinary opportunities for success. Everyone, of course, is different and each person requires a slightly different approach, but

I've learned there are certain body tactics we all can employ to make those connections. Each of us can develop skills to help us pass every dopamine test.

Kinetic Empathy

Have you ever noticed what people do with their hands? The next time you're standing in line to get into a movie or your favorite restaurant, pay attention to the body language of your fellow queue members. Some people will be gesturing, others constantly shifting their weight, some leaning in to make a point, others touching shoulders or arms. The interplay between body positions is a kind of language in itself, indicating all kinds of emotions, responses, intentions and degrees of intimacy. I've noticed that men and women assume very different body positions, and there seems to be a definite gender preference specifically revealed in hand and arm placement. It seems that women tend to cross their arms during pauses, while men are more likely to put their hands in their pockets to signal a break in the body conversation. The point is, we all adopt certain body language from our cultures and from the people around us. The subconscious positioning and gesturing carry with them definite messages that influence, project and reflect how we're feeling inside at any given moment. What you say with your body can invite intimacy and provide you with opportunities to connect in positive ways with other people.

As we've seen from studies cited earlier in this chapter, empathy is an important trait to express in the establishment of intimacy and the creation of a positive connection. I've learned to use my observations of body language to make connections with people and get them to open up to me quicker and in ways they probably would not otherwise have. Part of my job as principal of my marketing agency is to meet with business leaders to stay up to date on the needs of existing and potential clients and, of course, to convince them to give us work. Just as for you, my time is precious and I am able to devote only a small portion of my day to networking. Still, it's an important part of my business; without it, I'd be a lot less successful. So to make the most of my limited time, I use body language to help in communicating when I discuss the issues that will affect my agency now and in the future. The people I meet with don't have a lot of time to waste either, so they appreciate my ability to get right to the heart of the matter in a short time.

There's more to getting the information I need than just asking relevant questions. Simply verbalizing isn't enough to bridge the chasm that initially exists between all individuals. In fact, some questions are of such a delicate nature that to pose them without first creating the proper rapport can seem forward, even rude. The *way* I ask is as important as *what* I ask. That's because a certain amount of politics goes along with every job. There are often rivalries, turf battles and conflicting ideas about what needs to happen and how. It's important to root out these political machinations early on, but people are almost always hesitant to share that kind of information with anyone except those with whom they have close relationships. So a certain amount of intimacy is an important thing to develop, and I have to do it quickly.

I've discovered that most people have an unconscious tendency toward mimicry, or reflection, of body language. It's not something we think about, but it's there nonetheless. To illustrate this point, here's a little experiment you can try the next time you're having a conversation with someone. It could be a new acquaintance or a business colleague; your spouse, child or parent; or a complete stranger you meet at the coffee shop. It could even be someone toward whom you have romantic intentions. As you talk, pay attention to how the other person is standing or sitting. Is his or her posture erect, or is there a slight slouch at the shoulders? Is one foot in front of the other, or is the hip cocked at an angle? Now notice the hands. Do they hang loosely at the side or are they used to gesture? Are the arms crossed, or are the hands in the pockets? What about the head? Is it tilted to one side while listening? Do the hands come into contact with the face? Are the fingers run through the hair occasionally, or is there a little fiddling with the chin or nose? Is there movement inward when making an important point?

Now the fun begins. Start mimicking a gesture or two. When he or she shifts position, follow suit and change your position to match. Don't be too obvious about it, just work it in naturally. The next time he or she scratches the chin, scratch your chin, too. Pick up on as many fidgets, adjustments and nuances as you can. Continue to do this for a few minutes to get a rhythm going. Now, subtly begin to interject your own, different gestures. Stretch your arms wide and yawn, or look up at the sky and scratch your chin. You'll notice an amazing thing: After you've repeated your signature moves a few times, the other person will begin to imitate your exact movements. Within a few brief moments, you'll see the other person following your lead in almost everything you do. Subconsciously, you've indicated to the other person that you two have much in common, you've gotten the dopamine flowing. You take on the aura of empathy and gain a degree of respect and intimacy. You've turned an everyday moment into an opportunity to succeed. You've turned Your Three Second Window to your advantage and made contact. Now you can get down to work on exchanging relevant information in a more honest and complete manner.

A lot of my meetings happen over lunch. To get the other person's dopamine flowing even more and increase receptiveness, I'll ask what my guest's favorite food is. He or she will usually think for a moment or two, then smile and say lobster or sirloin steak, clam chowder or hot dogs. Regardless of what he or she finds most desirable, the reaction to thinking about good food is always a pleasurable one. The mere idea of a pleasant dining experience is, as far as the reward system is concerned, the same as actually eating that meal. The ventral tegmental area obligingly releases a measure of dopamine, and my guest experiences the welcome feeling we all share from having our human needs met. It should come as no surprise that when we are feeling good, we're more open to new ideas and experiences and more apt to connect with the other person. I find that when my guests are in this positive state of mind, communication is enhanced, we get a lot more done and both of us benefit. The whole interaction is like a tennis match in which both players win.

Connecting with Groups

A few years back, an agency I was with hired a new account person. Part of her job was to give what we call "capabilities presentations" to existing and potential clients. She would stand up in front of a group of marketing VPs and sing the praises of our company. She would show our work, talk about the talent, dazzle with our fantastic results. The presentation itself was developed by our creative team and, if I do say so myself, it was a knockout. But no matter how good the pictures, words, ideas and concepts are, selling still comes down to the person doing the talking. Now Judy (not her real name) was a very personable woman—attractive, lively, with a sense of enthusiasm that was hard to resist. Sitting around the office chatting, she was confident, at ease and full of interesting things to say. Still, for some reason, when she came back from the first few capabilities presentations, she seemed down, not her old bubbly self at all. "How'd the presentation go?" I'd ask.

"Not so good," she would sigh. "I guess I'm not much of a public speaker."

Few of us are born orators. In fact, in one survey, subjects ranked getting up in front of a group to speak as their number-one fear—above their number-two fear: death. Jerry Seinfeld remarked that this means attendees at a funeral would rather be the one in the coffin than the person giving the eulogy.

I understood perfectly how Judy felt. I remembered the terror I felt as a young teaching assistant the first time I had to teach a class on my own. I fretted about it for weeks and when the big day came, I had a lump in my throat the size of an orange. My palms were sweaty and I felt sick to my stomach. So many fears ran through my head: *What if I forget what I'm going to say? What if the students ask me a question I can't answer? What if I freeze up and can't speak at all?* All these bugaboos haunted me through the first few minutes of class. I nervously introduced myself, talked a bit about what the course would cover and outlined what would be expected of the students—all boilerplate stuff I'd heard my professors saying for the last five or six years. I was trying desperately to appear "professorial," striking casual, confident poses as I strove to control the fear burning inside me. Before class, I'd scouted the classroom and choreographed a couple of moves I thought would inspire the students' confidence in me. One of my moves involved casually pulling up a stool and sitting down while thoughtfully gazing upward and sagely pondering a question from one of my students. When the moment actually came and I casually pulled the stool up behind me, I failed to notice a box of pushpins left on the seat. I sat down and a couple of the wicked little devils poked through my trousers. I jumped up with a yelp, tipping over the stool, scattering the pins and frantically pulling brightly colored tacks from the seat of my pants.

Of course the classroom—all thirty or so students—erupted in wild laughter and, after a moment or two, I joined in. Talk about an icebreaker! After that little humiliation, I thought, *Well, it can't get worse than that!* I quit trying to put on a show and relaxed; to my surprise, the rest of the class was a pure delight. I'd already made a complete fool of myself, so nothing I could do would further damage my credibility. The curtain had come down, the façade had crumbled, the jig was up. I was a person, just like the rest of the people in class. I was completely at ease, and the class sensed it. The funny thing is, my minor embarrassment actually enhanced my status with my students. We were all a lot more relaxed and over the course of the quarter, we got a lot done. Students came up to me on the last day to say what fun they'd had and how much they'd learned. Quite a few of them signed up for my class the next quarter—and it all started in a funny little Three Second Window when, instead of running and hiding in humiliation, I took the opportunity to show a little grace, see the humor of it all and turn it to my advantage. I believe that the fact I was able to laugh at myself had an endearing effect and allowed me to better connect with my students every time I got up to teach the class.

Since that day, I've made hundreds of presentations and lectures to groups large and small and have always been able to connect with them right away. When I get up in front of a group to speak, I am comfortable, at ease and totally confident. Part of my confidence comes from knowing my material front and back, but an equal part comes from the knowledge that no matter what happens, nothing can be as embarrassing as sitting on a box of tacks.

But I digress; let's get back to Judy. One day, after about her third or fourth unsuccessful capabilities presentation, she cornered me in the hall. "What am I doing wrong?" she asked. "When I get up to speak, I feel so self-conscious." She shook her head. "I get the fear!"

"Get a box of pushpins," I said.

"What?!"

"Never mind. Listen," I told her, "there's a little trick I use. I stand in front of the group and don't say anything at all for about thirty seconds. People will be talking among themselves, checking their e-mail, doodling in their notepads. Just stand there, look out at each person and don't say a word until the room quiets down. Make eye contact. Don't rush it; believe me, they'll get the idea. While you're waiting for your audience to get in the right frame of mind, you need to get into the right frame of mind, too. You'll need to do a little pretending."

"Pretending?" Judy asked.

"Pretend everyone in that room is madly in love with you. I mean, really convince yourself that you are the most glamorous, witty and charismatic person in the world. Everyone wants to be you."

"Easier said than done," Judy smirked.

"I didn't say it would be easy, but once you get in that state of mind, you'll see it comes naturally. This mindset gives you an incredible amount of confidence, and your audience will pick up on it. They'll listen more closely and be more attentive, and their respect for what you have to say will increase. You'll sense it in the atmosphere and that will build up your confidence even more. It's an upward spiral. By the end of your presentation, you'll have your audience eating out of your hand, and no one—including you—will want it to end."

Judy's performance improved after our conversation and a little more coaching. She's since moved on to bigger and better things. I heard the other day that she has just been elected president of an industry organization and one of her duties is to run a monthly dinner meeting involving large groups. Good for you, Judy!

Sharing the Joy

I've always known that for good or bad, a bond of sorts develops between a speaker and his or her audience. Thinking back to the tack incident now, it makes a lot of sense that once we all shared a laugh and got the dopamine flowing, our connection would be a good, strong and long-lasting one.

We all understand that laughter and good feelings are contagious and help us make meaningful connections. As the ribald Elizabethan poem goes, "A maiden laughing is a maiden half taken!" But have you ever wondered why? What is it about seeing someone else enjoy life that brings happiness to us, too? Is it simply that we imagine ourselves in the other's position? Or is there some deeper, more mysterious interaction that occurs inside our brains and gives rise to the sense of joy we feel from the positive experiences of others? Do the physical cues, such as body language and facial expressions, that signal to the outside world the joyous internal state of another trigger the same in us? In my experience, the answer is yes. I know that when I speak to a group, I make a conscious effort to project positive physical cues—"good vibrations." Ninety-nine percent of the time, I see those positive physical cues reflected back to me, which reinforces my own positive state of mind, which in turn further stimulates my audience and so on. I understand that everyone in the audience is having their own Three Second Windows subjecting me to their individual dopamine tests, and I take advantage of that knowledge and use it to get them on my side. At times, I get an almost euphoric feeling when giving a presentation, no doubt the result of the production of large amounts of dopamine by my reward system. I'm simply using the connections between aesthetics and the pleasure and decision-making centers of the brain to create a positive and entertaining environment that invites success. Verbal and nonverbal cues are strong indicators of our internal states of mind; in a group, people will look to the speaker for signals about how they should be feeling. An energetic, engaging presenter will infect his or her audience with a sense of well-being, inclusion and enthusiasm, while a lethargic, remote speaker will create distance, disinterest and a sense of unease and disconnect.

Tuning In

Most communication happens subconsciously. Your subconscious is particularly good at picking out desirable traits in other people and rewarding your conscious brain with a shot of the feel-good chemical dopamine. Under the spell of dopamine, you get the sense that your human needs are being met; you think, *I like this person.* While very few encounters will result in love at first sight, you can still use your understanding of the phenomenon of instant attraction and Your Three Second Window to create positive connections and momentum in your favor. Whether you're interacting with another individual or with a group, the same principles apply. Confidence, empathy, joie de vivre, grace and a sprinkling of attitude are all admirable human traits when used in the correct measure, and they go a long way toward creating positive connections and opportunities for success.

Chapter 2

The Beauty of Success

In today's hectic, results-driven environment we often—in the interest of productivity and the bottom line—make an artificial distinction between utility and beauty, when in truth the two are inseparable. People and things that produce the release of dopamine—pass the dopamine test—are better at what they do. A person you find attractive is going to get your attention faster and hold it longer and so can accomplish more. A product that is aesthetically pleasing is more enjoyable to use than one that you perceive as ugly. People and things that stimulate your reward system (all other things being equal) function at a higher level because they provide more enjoyment for your life. And that makes you more creative, productive and efficient. As children, we all possessed an instinctive appreciation for beauty. In a few, it remained and even grew, but for too many of us, the ability to consciously recognize beauty and its effect, the production of dopamine, has been trained out of us. It's time to relearn what has been lost.

To take advantage of every Three Second Window, you need to acknowledge and accept the advantages that beauty provides. Learning to consciously recognize beauty and the rush of dopamine it generates is the first step toward being able to project your own personal beauty, surround yourself with beauty and impart beauty into the things you make. When you do, you are much happier and more successful in all the spheres of your life.

This observation is nothing new. Ancient humans understood the connection between aesthetics and pleasure, and yes, the utility it provides.

All through history, beauty has played a key role in every aspect of human life. From religion and politics to business and industry, at work and at home, in private and in the public square, the presence of beauty is often the deciding factor between success and failure, survival and extinction. An appreciation of beauty and a desire to create it are ingrained in our genetic makeup; it's one of the things that makes us human and has contributed to our survival as a species.

Beauty inspires us to greatness and to sacrifice and drives our strongest desires. It stands out and is instantly recognizable. It's what stimulates our reward systems and makes every Three Second Window work. To learn to recognize Your Three Second Windows and turn them to your advantage, you must first understand how important beauty is, how it functions and the role it plays in turning everyday moments into extraordinary opportunities for success.

The History of Beauty

We have evolved to appreciate beauty as a survival technique. Beauty helps us sort the survival benefits from the threats. We see genetically suitable members of the opposite sex as potential mates, which is a way of saying we see them as beautiful. A verdant meadow with grazing game is a place where abundance thrives and so it is beautiful. They pass our dopamine tests. A barren stretch of desert devoid of food and water does not.

A misconception about beauty is that it is mysterious and indefinable. In fact, there are long-established concepts of what constitutes beauty or at least what makes up the aesthetic experience. The art of creating and appreciating beauty is as old as humankind itself. As we've seen from the last chapter, beauty plays a key role in communicating genetic appropriateness through fitness indicators. It's important to communicating in other ways, too. Early people were very much concerned with the look of the things they made. Ritualistic paintings, sculptures, talismans, fetishes and even tools had to meet certain aesthetic requirements to be considered useful. That beauty was so important to our ancestors speaks to the raw power of the aesthetic experience. Ancient people needed beauty in their lives because it served utilitarian purposes, a fact often lost in modern life.

The Hunter

> In some scrawny troop of beleaguered not-yet-men on some
> scrawny forgotten plain, a radian particle from an unknown
> source fractured a never-to-be-forgotten gene, and a primate
> carnivore was born. For better or for worse, for tragedy or for
> triumph, for ultimate glory or ultimate damnation, intelligence
> made alliance with the way of the killer, and Cain with his
> sticks and his stones and his quickly running feet emerged on
> the high savannah. Abel stayed behind in the bush.
>
> —From African Genesis by Robert Ardrey

Imagine the Stone Age hunting party. A group of six or eight men dressed in animal skins and furs, meager protection indeed from the bitter cold sweeping out of the icy heights and down across the plains. They've been following the bison for days now; the party is spread out along the perimeter of the herd, directing it with shouts and waving arms into the canyon where the hulking animals will bunch up and the men will make their kills. The hunters are equipped with the latest weapons their technology can provide: pointed sticks and rocks. The bison are huge, weighing hundreds of pounds with horns growing to three feet. In close, the way the hunters will be making their kills, the bison can be dangerous, even deadly. The possibility of being gored or trampled to death is real and the hunters know it all too well. Now the herd is where the hunting party wants it. The animals are nervous, they sense the men's presence and they're on the verge of stampede. Once the killing begins, the smell of blood will drive them wild with fear and anything can happen. Death is near now. The men trade nervous glances, grip their sticks and rocks a little tighter and begin to close in.

Hunting was a necessity for our Stone Age ancestors. The tribe needed food to survive and the huge herds of herbivores roaming the ancient plains were sometimes the only sources. It took a lot of courage and determination to do battle with the big animals. Days and weeks of unbelievable hardships might lead to plenty or just as likely to a hunter's death on the cold ground. The hope of a full stomach was certainly a good reason to attend the hunt, but our ancient ancestors had other, equally powerful forms of motivation, too.

Art of the Old Stone Age (Late Paleolithic) represents a millennia-old tradition. It's in the earlier part of this period that we see humans creating tools. Toward the end of the Late Paleolithic, about 15,000 to 10,000 B.C., we begin to see other, more sophisticated art forms emerge. Perhaps the most famous of these Late Paleolithic examples are the cave paintings at Lascaux in the Dordogne region of France. The Lascaux cave paintings are very lifelike in their brightly colored representations of bison, deer, horses and cattle. They had to be, because they served a vital function in inspiring our ancient hunter ancestors. Archaeologists believe they were probably an important part of hunting rituals in which the painted animals were symbolically killed. In his book *History of Art,* H.W. Janson writes of the cave paintings at Lascaux:

> There can be little doubt, in fact, that they were produced as part of a magic ritual, perhaps to ensure a successful hunt. We gather this not only from their secret location, and from the lines meant to represent spears or darts that are sometimes found pointing at the animals, but also from the peculiar way the images are superimposed on one another. Apparently, people of the Old Stone Age made no clear distinction between image and reality; by making a picture of an animal, they meant to bring the animal itself within their grasp, and in 'killing' the image they thought they had killed the animal's vital spirit. Hence a 'dead' image lost its potency after the killing ritual had been performed, and could be disregarded when the spell had to be renewed.

It could be said that advertising is the cave painting of the twenty-first century. In the same way our ancestors created images to motivate and inspire, today's advertising images are created to get us to buy. Instead of braving the wilderness and ferocious animals, we brave the freeways and aisles of our supermarkets. Still, the single most important motivating force behind all human behavior remains the same: survival. Although ads today are technically more sophisticated and reach a larger audience, their roots go back to that earlier time and are based on the same sense of aesthetics that got our prehistoric ancestors to take action. We are still tempted with images of attractive and desirable people and things: cars, homes, food, all those necessities of life plus a lot that's not so necessary. Think about an ad you've seen recently. Odds are it used some kind of visual stimulation, an image of some sort to get you to imagine possessing the thing. It's an age-old technique used to get your dopamine flowing just the way those cave paintings did for Paleolithic man.

Those cave paintings were intended to get our ancestors to imagine possessing the animal that was the object of the hunt. Killing the painting was tantamount to ensuring an actual kill. If the cave paintings did a good job of capturing the life spirit of the animals they represented, the hunt was more likely to be successful. It's not much of a stretch of the imagination to see how our hunting party, filled with confidence from the symbolic kill, would show increased bravery and skill in the actual hunt. But for the images to work their magic, the hunters had to feel an immediate emotional response. They had to perceive beauty. They needed to experience the essence of the animal and a desire to possess it. They needed to have their own Three Second Windows.

Creating such powerful images must have been no small effort and surely took much skill and training in the techniques of drawing and in the cultural traditions surrounding the hunting rituals. The artists who painted the animals at Lascaux were certainly talented, but their images did not suddenly spring into existence as the product of one artist's inspiration. They were no doubt based on a long cultural and aesthetic tradition reaching back thousands of years. Their fathers and their fathers' fathers had probably been motivated by similar images during similar rituals and had gone forth to do battle with wild beasts, too. The Stone Age hunters believed in the power of their images to influence the outcome of events outside the ritual because they fit the aesthetic and cultural requirements—the definitions of beauty—developed over the ages and passed down from generation to generation. If the images didn't feel right, if they didn't have a certain kind of beauty, the magic wouldn't work. But if the paintings expressed the beauty of the real animal in life, the ritual would be successful. Talk about a tough bunch of art critics.

The Lascaux paintings are uniquely of their place and time. They show the ingenuity of early man in his attempts to control his own destiny. The cave paintings were important, so they had to be right. The cave artists were working with very basic tools and techniques: sticks for brushes, crude dyes for paint and living stone for canvas. But these limitations seemed only to challenge, not defeat, the attempts of these early artists at capturing the beauty and the spirit of the animals they portrayed. Many of the Lascaux paintings use natural features of the rock as integral parts of the images. Often an image seems to follow naturally occurring bumps, lines, cracks and veins of rock. In that way, the artist would "find" the animal's image in the rock wall of the cave. It took a sharp eye and active imagination to spot these natural clues and create whole images from them. These attributes, combined with his importance to the existence of the tribe, no doubt gave the artist a position of high social status among his fellow tribesmen. Again, from H.W. Janson: "It is tempting to think that those who proved particularly good at finding such images were given a special status as artist-magicians and were relieved of the dangers of the real hunt so that they could perfect their image-hunting, until finally they learned how to make images with little or no aid from chance formations, though they continued to welcome such aid."

Today we see evident in the Lascaux cave paintings a very sophisticated understanding of visual principles of beauty and the aesthetic experience: scale, proportion, texture and form. Still, we might think of the ancient hunter as primitive in his need for beauty as a source of inspiration and motivation. Yet are we modern humans that much different? Aren't we still moved to heroic deeds by beauty? Several thousand years after those brave hunters stalked herds of bison on the plains to ensure the survival of their tribe, another group of humans, inspired by a different expression of beauty, rallied to a great cause and had a monumental effect that shaped *their* world, too.

South Pacific

The island war was dragging on. Four years of bitter struggle in Europe and the Pacific had strained the resources of America to the breaking point. The Germans and Italians would soon be defeated, but the Japanese struggled on. It would take a much greater effort and huge sums of money to defeat the Pacific enemy, and the U.S. government was nearly broke. Unless the next war bond drive was able to generate many billions of dollars, total defeat of the Empire of the Rising Sun might not be possible. President Truman might have to sue for a settled peace. The American public had already responded to a number of appeals and had given generously. It seemed there just wasn't that much left to give. Something dramatic would have to happen to motivate a war-weary nation to rally to the call. There would need to be a collective Three Second Window involving millions of people before the terrible war could be brought to a successful conclusion. The dramatic event that saved the day turned out to be not so dramatic—at least to the U.S. Marines on Iwo Jima. To the American public, however, the impact was to be much different.

The best-selling book by James Bradley, *Flags of Our Fathers*, tells the story of the raising of the American flag on Iwo Jima by U.S. Marines during World War II. The famous photograph stirred a nation's soul. Of an Independence Day celebration in Washington, D.C., James Bradley writes:

> On the night of July 4, the capital was a tumult of the rockets' red glare, the bombs bursting in air. Some 350,000 spectators—a larger crowd even than would assemble for Martin Luther King's March on Washington eighteen years later—turned their faces upward to watch fireworks explode and spread their contrails over the Washington Monument, turning the Potomac's surface, for nearly an hour, into a mirror of reds and whites and yellows and greens. The fireworks filled the night sky with the outlines of the American flag, the face of President Truman, and the Iwo Jima flag raising scene.

When the Iwo Jima photo was first published in newspapers across the country, people were moved in very deep and profound ways and the money generated by the associated bond drive contributed greatly to the American victory over the Empire of Japan. From *Flags of Our Fathers*: "The tour had not just met its goal; the tour had nearly doubled it: Americans had pledged $26.3 billion. This was equal to almost half of the 1946 total U.S. government budget of $56 billion." Later in his book, Bradley writes:

> An Iwo Jima commemorative stamp was issued on July 11, the anniversary of the founding of the Marine Corps Reserve.

It was the first stamp to feature living people. Even Presidents had to die to get their image on a stamp. It immediately broke post office records for first-day sales, topping 400,000. In time, 150 million stamps would be printed, making it the bestselling stamp in history up to that time.

Even today, for most people, the image of the Marines on Iwo Jima elicits an instant and strong emotional response. It could be said *that simple photograph did more to win the war than even the atomic bomb.* In its ability to touch people in very meaningful ways, the Iwo Jima image is not unlike the cave paintings at Lascaux. Both motivated their audiences to take action. In the case of the cave paintings, the action was to go out and slay animals to provide food for the tribe. In the case of the Iwo Jima photo, citizens were motivated to buy war bonds and provide money to further support America's struggle against Japan. In both cases, groups of people experienced Three Second Windows leading to actions critical to the survival of their respective societies.

So, what is it about the Iwo Jima photograph and the Lascaux paintings that gave them such power to motivate their respective audiences? Both the Lascaux cave paintings and the Iwo Jima photo generally fulfill our need for aesthetic satisfaction. They both were strongly connected to issues vital to the survival of their cultures and observed their own visual and ritualistic traditions. It's the aesthetic qualities, though, that first catch our eyes and pass our dopamine tests and it's the way they each linked the viewers to their times that gave them both their meaning and their power to motivate and unite.

As we've seen, the cave paintings probably played an important part in hunting rituals. The images of bison, deer, cattle and other animals had magical connotations to the ancient hunters. The images would have meant successful hunting, a time of plenty and continued existence for the tribe. We can say with more certainty what meaning the Iwo Jima image had to an American World War II audience. Accounts of the time make reference to the photo stirring feelings of patriotism, victory over a formidable enemy, progress in a long, drawn-out war and pride in the accomplishments of American troops.

As meaningful as the Iwo Jima photo was, and still is, it's the picture's visual appeal—its beauty—that accounts for its initial power to inspire. Ironically, if not for the trained eye of an artist who happened to spot the photo during routine editing of pictures, it might never have come to light. According to Bradley's book, Navy Petty Officer Felix de Weldon was stationed at Patuxent Naval Air Station when he first saw the now-famous Iwo Jima photo. Dr. de Weldon was educated in the fine arts, having studied European painting and sculpture. The photo stopped him in his tracks. Bradley writes, "In its classical triangular lines, he recognized similarities with the ancient statues he had studied." Felix de Weldon responded instantly to the beauty of the image. His reward system recognized certain visual qualities, produced a shot of dopamine and informed his conscious brain that this was something he needed to pay attention to. It was a genuine Three Second Window.

Discovering Beauty in Everyday Moments

We're all able to appreciate obvious examples of beauty. We marvel at a spectacular sunset, sense the peace of the ocean rhythms, are lost in the gaze of a loved one. We find joy and completion in beauty, an inner satisfaction that defies description. Beauty plays an important part in the enjoyment of our lives, yet most of us experience it so rarely. It seems, in this modern world, we think of beauty as a luxury, something to be enjoyed only in our idle or leisure moments. Few of us incorporate the joy of beauty into the fabric of our everyday lives. What a shame, because the joy of beauty is closely intertwined with success in all aspects of life.

I was having a drink with a friend at a bar one evening, many summers ago now, when I looked out the window and was enthralled by the quality of the setting sun's light on the leaves of a tree. I called this wonderful phenomenon to the attention of my companion. She glanced at the tree, studied it for a few moments, then turned to me with a quizzical expression. "I don't see anything beautiful about that," she said.

I was stunned that she was unable, or perhaps unwilling, to experience the joy of beauty in that everyday moment. The truth is, just as each day is filled with Three Second Windows, each moment can be one in which we experience the joy of beauty. Beauty doesn't have to be reserved for special occasions. Its domain is not exclusively that of the museum or salon.

I think the problem my friend had in seeing the beauty in that tree that day was rooted in her idea of what beauty is. We are conditioned to think of beauty as something rare, some spectacular natural event or a masterwork by a great artist—and it can be. But it's also a lot more common and accessible than that. So let's redefine beauty a little so that we can learn to recognize it and its effect: the release of dopamine. Let's practice making beauty a bigger part of our lives.

Try this simple exercise to help you recognize the presence of beauty and the associated shot of dopamine it produces: Take a look at your hands: their shape, texture, the amazing dexterity of the wrists and fingers. Turn them palms up and examine closely the fine lines and creases, the intricate patterns and whorls. Now hold them up and turn them slowly so that the light plays upon their shapes. Observe how the shadows move, dissipate and reform as you rotate your hands through the light. Now acknowledge the beauty you are experiencing. Right now, your subconscious brain is producing a shot of dopamine and sending a signal to your consciousness that your human needs are being met. Feels good, doesn't it? This simple exercise helps you see the beauty that surrounds you if you just allow yourself the pleasure. Now look around. If you're outside, notice the sky, the trees, the way the wind blows the grass. Even a hurtling taxicab, a blowing plastic bag or smoke rising from a chimney can be beautiful when looked at with the right set of eyes. If you're indoors, notice the play of light and shadow against a wall or the shape of a houseplant or piece of furniture. Make it a point to find beauty in every moment. Practice letting your reward system release that dopamine. Learn to administer the dopamine test and recognize its presence even when it's just a tiny trace. At first you'll have to look for it, but soon you'll experience it without effort; it will become part of the fabric of your life and it will enrich your days in ways you never imagined.

Appreciating beauty in every way teaches you to recognize the feeling of dopamine so you can practice stimulating your and others' reward systems, create your own Three Second Windows and change those everyday moments into extraordinary opportunities for success.

As we saw in Chapter 1, modern technology has provided us with the means to map the enjoyment of beauty—the aesthetic experience—as it occurs in our brains. Scientists are able to pinpoint the common structures, chemicals and systems that make us feel good when we experience beauty. Still, that experience is an intensely personal one that moves us in deep and powerful ways. Maybe that's why we humans have always felt a need for beauty and a drive to create it when it's missing in our lives. We've even come up with principles and rules about how to make things beautiful. The search for a universal method of creating beauty has been going on for as long as we have been human, and it continues today. But why do we crave the aesthetic experience so? I suspect it can be traced simply to our natural desire to feel good. Experiencing beauty is similar to the feeling of a full stomach or a warm fire—the feeling of that little shot of dopamine that comes when our subconscious brains signal us that our basic human needs are being met. In other words, it all comes down to emotion.

But in some cases, experiencing beauty can lead to much more than just a good feeling. It can inspire us to great things. Homer tells us that Helen of Troy had a "face that launched a thousand ships." Her beauty was so great, myth says, that nations went to war over her. The drive to accomplish great things in the service of a higher purpose is different than the drive to fulfill our everyday needs or to satisfy some immediate want, such as the purchase of a new car. There exists a kind of motivation that transcends personal comfort, security and sometimes our own self-interest and well-being. There's something inside us all that strives for greatness, but it takes a powerful force to arouse and direct it toward some noble end. It can't be done without beauty.

As we have seen, instant attraction plays a key role in all kinds of motivation: motivation to seek a mate, motivation to make a purchase, motivation to come to a decision. Perhaps the most powerful role it plays, though, is in motivating individuals and whole groups of people to dedicate energy, forego comfort and make significant, even supreme, sacrifices for a cause. Beauty has been used over the ages to motivate people to achieve great things—for themselves and, through altruism, for others. Beauty can awaken the sleeping hero in all of us.

The Dopamine-Powered Climb

My first climb of a big mountain took place in the summer of 1975. I'd signed up with the local guide service, Rainier Mountaineering Incorporated, for a six-day climbing course; the "final exam" was an ascent of Washington State's fourteen-thousand-four-hundred and ten foot-high Mount Rainier. The training was rigorous, covering rope handling, knots, glacier travel and crevasse rescue. Physical training in preparation for the climb was strenuous, involving long runs, weight lifting and almost daily excursions carrying a forty-pound backpack up and down the hills in and around Seattle. But when the big day came, I was ready. I shouldered my pack and in the company of the other novice climbers and our trusty guides, started up the Muir Snowfield on the south flank of Mount Rainier. It would be a steep, five-hour-long slog from the parking lot at five thousand feet to Camp Muir at ten thousand feet, where we'd spend the first night.

I was only twenty-five years old and in great shape, and still I found the climb to Camp Muir tough. It was a scorching-hot July day and the sun beat down mercilessly on our heads. The rays, reflecting on the snow, were sunburning every bit of exposed flesh, even the insides of our ears and nostrils. As we climbed higher and the air grew thinner, it became more difficult to breathe. We had been taught a special technique called pressure breathing that allows for greater absorption of oxygen into the lungs to compensate for the rarefied atmosphere. Pressure breathing involves gulping in as much air as possible, filling and expanding the lungs to their greatest capacity, then pursing the lips and forcing the air out as though blowing up a balloon. It works, but it takes a lot of energy and by the time we reached Camp Muir, I was exhausted.

At high altitude, unless you are completely acclimated, you are always short of breath, thirsty, nauseated and headachy. Your thought process slows down to the point where carrying on a conversation is a strenuous task. Simple things such as dressing or undressing become a weighty effort. Sleeping can be next to impossible; I remember waking up several times that first night gasping for air. I needn't have worried too much about sleep, though, because at midnight the guides rousted us out of our sleeping bags to go for the summit.

It was dark and cold, and a bitter wind blew down off the upper mountain as we crunched along on the hard snow, our crampons biting into the firm surface, the light from our headlamps casting eerie shadows on the moonlit snow. As hard as the trip to Camp Muir had been, this was much worse. My feet were freezing, my hands gripping the ice axe were numb. I was afraid to look down into the gaping crevasses, big enough it seemed in that beautiful, silvery light to swallow a whole city block. I was cold, tired, sick and scared. *What am I doing here?* I thought as I puffed my way up and past the Disappointment Cleaver, a giant rock outcropping topping out at more than twelve thousand feet above sea level. It wasn't long before I got my answer.

The sun rises early in July that high on the mountain. It was about four-thirty or a quarter to five when the first rays broke over the Cascade Mountains to our south and east. We'd stopped for a water break; I had scooped out a little seat in the snow and was trying to force down a square of chocolate for the energy value when the whole mountain below me turned from silver and black to wheaten gold. I watched in stunned fascination as the sun's rays bathed the glaciers in amber light, the sky going from pure, star-studded black to a shade of azure I hadn't known existed. I thought back to when I'd first been bitten by the bug to climb Mount Rainier. During a shopping trip to Recreational Equipment Incorporated—REI—in Seattle, a poster of the mountain had caught my eye and passed the dopamine test in a big way. It was a glorious, full-color photo of a summer sunrise taken, it now seemed, from this very same spot! That poster had motivated me all right. But it wasn't to buy something, it was to accomplish something: a great feat, the realization of which would be in doubt until the very moment I stood on the summit. It had been a memorable Three Second Window.

My journey up the mountain had begun that day in REI when the poster captivated me. The image tugged at some deep, emotional thread and I was hooked. It wasn't long after when I signed up for the climbing course that would lead me to this magical place on this most unusual of days. A simple image had motivated me to begin a physical, mental and emotional journey requiring great sacrifice, hard work and dedication to an avocation that would change my life forever.

I was not alone that day. There were ten or twelve other people feeling the same effects of altitude, oxygen deprivation, lack of sleep, fatigue and thirst. Yet they were there. Each of us had a need to climb the mountain. For some, the motivation was an image like the one that touched me that day at REI; for others, it might have been another person who provided the impetus or it could have simply been the beauty of the idea of standing atop that grand peak that drove them.

I remember turning to my rope mate that morning. Words were unnecessary. We just smiled. Later that day, returning from the summit, we passed strolling tourists on the lower mountain paths a mile or so from the parking lot. We were sunburned and haggard looking; climbing ropes, crampons and ice axes dangled from our enormous packs as we trudged along. We pretended not to notice the admiring looks of the day hikers as we filed past, each of us exhibiting an almost military bearing. We were proud; we had accomplished a great feat. We were *motivated.* To this day, I wonder if any one of those tourists, inspired by our wizened countenances, became mountain climbers. Did we create a Three Second Window for someone else that afternoon?

The beautiful color photograph that immediately captured my attention at REI was the starting point of a long spiritual and professional journey. That morning on the glacier, when I was transfixed by the amazing light show of sun and ice, instilled in me a new appreciation for the beauty of nature, and I became seriously interested in photography. In time, photography led me to graphic design, to a rewarding academic and commercial career and finally to the writing of this book. Quite an achievement for a little shot of dopamine.

There's a slumbering hero inside us all. It could be an image, a place, an idea or another person that awakens us to heed the call of a great cause. The cause could be a personal goal, such as the scaling of a mountain or the acquisition of an advanced degree. It might be a collective goal, like raising money for a charity or even winning a war. Whether personal or collective, the accomplishment of lofty goals always calls for effort and commitment and sometimes for great sacrifice. Perhaps that's why this kind of motivation is not easily created in most of us. The greater the cause, the greater the effort and sacrifice, the greater the power of motivation must be.

Beauty comes in all shapes and forms. It might be an outward physical aesthetic that inspires, it might be some inner attractiveness that moves us;

most often it is some combination of both. Only a few possess the power that comes from beauty to motivate people to achieve great things. How do they do it? What special talents do they own? How are they able to awaken the slumbering heroes within each of us?

"The Only Thing We Have to Fear Is Fear Itself"

Few presidents so motivated the country in time of crisis as did Franklin D. Roosevelt. With the bombing of Pearl Harbor on December 7, 1941, and the subsequent American entrance into the Pacific and European wars, FDR rallied a nation to save Western democracy from the dictatorships of Tojo, Hitler and Mussolini. Stricken with polio and for the most part confined to a wheelchair, FDR directed the course of history through his masterful use of charm, his charisma and his uncanny ability to connect with people, communicate his point of view and win support for his policies. FDR had discovered his own unique kind of beauty and learned how to create Three Second Windows to motivate others.

During the war, a huge military buildup made resources scarce for the average American. Factories that had been producing automobiles were now building armaments, creating a shortage of cars for civilian use. Steel, rubber, gasoline, oil, meat, vegetables, butter, coffee, sugar and just about everything else you can think of were rationed. Just about the only things in abundance were the president's wit, buoyant optimism and paternal guidance. Since his first term in 1932, FDR had been giving his Fireside Chats over the radio regularly. Continuing through the war, his reassuring voice was heard in the evenings by millions of Americans, keeping them informed about the progress of our armies overseas and asking for still more sacrifice from his listeners. To save fuel and rubber, Roosevelt asked them to limit their driving. To conserve food, he asked Americans to plant Victory Gardens. His plea to citizens to buy war bonds was answered over and over again as Americans, from youngsters to the elderly, invested their meager savings in a struggle the results of which were far from certain.

Civilian life during World War II was one of shared hardship and sacrifice with no end in sight. The news from the front was not always encouraging, but even in the darkest days of the conflict, FDR never lost his good humor or his ability to motivate a nation to reach loftier goals.

My mother was working in an airplane factory in California during the war. She talked about the hardships of the home front: the lack of adequate housing, stark rationing of everyday essentials and the generally Spartan living conditions the vagaries of war demanded. Yet she also spoke of an enduring admiration for FDR, and she seemed not a little wistful for that time when one man, frail of health but robust in spirit, brought a nation together and marshaled its collective will toward the achievement of a noble cause.

When I asked my mother how FDR managed to communicate so well and motivate so completely, she answered, "He didn't talk down to you on those radio shows he used to have. He made us feel important and absolutely necessary. Back in that time, we all felt a part of one big family." Roosevelt grew up wealthy, but developed a common touch that resonated with the average woman and man. "I was young then, and I felt that as long as he was leading us, we'd be all right. Nothing ever got him down and it made me feel good to do the things he asked. We were all in it together," my mother said.

FDR truly awoke the slumbering hero, not in just a few, but in an entire generation. He inspired millions by incorporating all the X-factors into his personality to create Three Second Windows for a nation—but he had more going for him than that. He was an attractive man with a chiseled jaw, a robust chest, a lion's mane of hair and wit and intelligence that shone through even in the toughest times. He could be said to exhibit perfectly the masculine ideal of beauty. Because of his polio, his withered legs would not support him for long and most of his time was spent in a wheelchair. His infirmity, though, didn't diminish his appeal. He was an impeccable dresser and wore clothes that emphasized his attributes and played down his physical deformity. In many ways, FDR learned how to play the hand he'd been dealt to his and his nation's greatest advantage.

Discovering Your Own Beauty

A good friend of mine used to tell a funny story about the philosophy he followed in raising his two children. "Well," he said, "I've made them afraid of the dark, now all I have to do is make them ashamed of their bodies." He of course was kidding, but his joke is all the funnier because it is based in a truth about how we have come to think about our bodies. Locker rooms, the bedroom and hospitals aside, there are few times and places where most of us would be comfortable being seen nude, no matter how in shape we might be. We are raised to be modest, and this modesty is reflected in how we think about our bodies. Our own evaluation of our appearance is by definition highly subjective, so it can be difficult to accurately gauge what impression our appearance will make on others. This sometimes makes it hard for us to recognize the beauty we all possess.

Throughout time, the human body has been a subject of great interest in many ways: scientifically, socially and of course sexually. One of the big questions about the body is how we see it. Do we consider our bodies as synonymous with ourselves or as something we possess? The answer is probably both. How we see our bodies depends on how we are thinking about them at the time. For instance, if you go to the gym and you and your personal trainer talk about strengthening your legs and arms, you will probably see your body as composed of different parts and something slightly separate from "self." You are viewing your legs and arms from the outside, as something to be analyzed and improved upon. In this case, your legs and arms are things that belong to you, but they are not you. On the other hand, if after your workout you indulge in a relaxing massage, the overall good feeling you get will probably tend to make you see your body as synonymous to yourself, with no separation between it and you. In this case, you and your body are one and the same.

How you see your relationship to your body plays an important role in how you project your own personal brand of beauty. If you fuss about your waist being too thick or your shoulders too slouchy, you're likely to carry that angst into your relationships with other people. And sure as the sun rises, they'll pick up on it. When we focus on our perceived imperfections and attempt to camouflage them, we are actually drawing attention to them. That's because nothing is more obvious than something you're trying to hide. Instead of attempting to disguise those things you imagine are wrong, think about your body as a whole instead of a conglomeration of mismatched parts. There's nothing wrong with trying to improve your conditioning and health, but remember that other people see you as a whole person, so it's important to think of yourself that way, too. Set the stage for successful interactions with others by being genuine and authentic in the way you dress and present yourself. Being who you are will take you a lot farther than any façade or costume.

Still, in this age of consumerism, it is common to think of our bodies as works in progress, things to be sculpted and made stronger, slimmer, fitter. In her book *The Fashioned Body*, Joanne Entwistle writes:

> The body has become the focus for increasing "work" (exercise, diet, make-up, cosmetic surgery, etc.) and there is a general tendency to see the body as part of one's self that is open to revision, change, transformation. The growth of healthy lifestyle regimes is testament to this idea that our bodies are unfinished, open to change. Exercise manuals and videos promise transformation of our stomachs, our hips, and thighs and so on. We are no longer content to see the body as finished, but actively intervene to change its shape, alter its weight and contours. The body has become part of a project to be worked at, a project increasingly linked to a person's identity of self. The care of the body is not simply about health, but about feeling good; increasingly, our happiness and personal fulfillment are pinned on the degree to which our bodies conform to contemporary standards of health and beauty.

Along with how we see our bodies is the issue of gender and sexuality. Men and women tend to have different views of the importance of how their bodies look. There's a lot more pressure on women to present an appropriate image to the world. Entwistle refers to John Berger's observation that "consciousness of bodily appearance is gendered: Berger has suggested that women more than men view their bodies as objects to be 'looked at' and this may indeed inform the choices women make when getting dressed for some situations." Society also tends to ascribe more of a moral connotation to the dress of women than to the dress of men. We are more likely to pass judgment on a woman's character based on her clothes. For instance, we might think of a woman with a short skirt as having looser morals than a woman whose dress ends below the knee. We rarely make such judgments about men based on the way they dress.

Ken Gilbert, M.D., is a board-certified plastic surgeon with a practice in the Boston area. He's a talented surgeon with twenty years in the field and has a lot of firsthand experience with how people view their bodies. When I spoke with him about the differences in how women and men see themselves, he had this to say: "About eighty-five percent of my elective patients are women. I think women have a lot more pressure put on them by society to look good. They tend to be more critical about their appearances than men. Men, on the other hand, often think they look good no matter what, and there's some physiological basis for that. You see, men have thicker skin and better blood supply, so they tend to show aging less than women."

I asked Dr. Gilbert if the patients he sees have a realistic body image. "I'd say for the most part, yes. One thing, though; we all tend to be more critical about the way we look than are the people around us. We spend a lot more time looking at ourselves than other people do. I see some patients who have unreal expectations, or come to me with problems surgery can't correct." Dr. Gilbert paused and went on. "And then there are some patients who have totally unrealistic body images; in fact, there's even a psychological condition called body dysmorphic disorder, where the patient blows a minor flaw all out of proportion or even believes that he or she is deformed when no actual deformity exists. It's rare, but I've seen a couple of patients with this condition. They are often addicted to plastic surgery and will go from doctor to doctor to try to get their imaginary problems fixed. People suffering from anorexia nervosa suffer from this condition."

Intense scrutiny of our bodies often results in insecurity born of a quest for a perfection that simply doesn't exist. While certain ideals of beauty are timeless, an overly detailed and defined prescription can lead to odd imagery. In ancient Egypt, for instance, a canon of proportions existed to describe the perfect body. Sculptors were required to follow this canon when creating statues of the pharaohs and their queens. In Mesopotamia, a different ideal existed for the perfect body, and it is reflected in statuary from that period. While these works of art possess an unquestionable beauty, they nonetheless look a little off to the modern eye.

Very few of us have bodies that fit the mold of perfection dictated by our time and culture, and striving for that ephemeral gold standard is almost always fruitless, leading only to frustration, a sense of inferiority and, sometimes, bizarre results. Just look at celebrities who have had extensive plastic surgery to "perfect" themselves to see what I mean. It's much more valuable and conducive to success to understand the basic, timeless qualities of beauty we all possess and work to emphasize them in ways that make us stand out as unique individuals, comfortable in our own skins. That way we can create our own, genuine Three Second Windows that truly open the way for success.

The way we see our bodies has a big influence on the clothes we choose to wear. The truth is, clothes aren't really clothes until we put them on. Hanging in the closet or folded in a drawer, they are simply stitched-together scraps of material. When seen hanging on a mannequin in a store window, they can even become a little creepy. But when we put clothes on, we literally bring them to life; we lend them our vitality, sense of style and personality. Just as we animate our clothes, they in turn influence how we feel and sometimes even how we behave.

Social scientists make a study of how we dress and the way our clothes affect how we act. Their studies have generated some interesting theories that shed light on why we choose the clothes we do. One theory posed by the sociologist Erving Goffman is particularly useful in creating a look for success. He coined the term "dramaturgy" to suggest that we go through life as actors on a stage, changing our looks and our actions to fit different places and times. In his book *The Presentation of Self in Everyday Life*, he uses the theater as a metaphor for the way we interact with other people: We are the actors, the places we go are the stages and the people around us are the audiences. Back stage is where we prepare ourselves for our front-stage performances. Back stage, we don our costumes, rehearse and get into character. Front stage is where we act out our roles, deliver our lines, tell our stories and create our Three Second Windows. Clothes become an important language in the telling of our stories—stories that usually change to some degree from time to time, place to place and audience to audience. While we all have our own personal roles to play, culture provides part of the script. The expectations of our audiences will determine to some degree the way we play our parts. For instance, those playing the role of a lawyer are expected to dress in certain ways, while expectations are different for those playing the role of an artist and different again for those who play police detectives. If those expectations are not rewarded, the credibility of the player will be suspect.

Consider this illustration of how our dress impacts the believability of our stories: A few winters ago, I was traveling through Europe with a friend. We were in and out of airports, train stations, hotels and restaurants and, without fail, the people we met immediately identified my friend as an American. They automatically spoke to him in English. They weren't fooled. But when I encountered Europeans on my own, no such assumption was made. They spoke to me in their native language.

My friend and I commented on this phenomenon and wondered how Europeans could pick my pal out as a Yankee, but often mistook me for one of their own. We have similar complexions, are about the same build and were dressed more or less alike. Finally, as I followed my friend through a train station one day, I figured it out. Looking around, I noticed a small detail I'd missed before. Suddenly I too could pick out the Americans in the crowd, fast and accurately. What do you think it was? The Americans were the only ones wearing running shoes. The Europeans, like me, were wearing some variation on more formal, leather footgear. Because my friend's "costume" wasn't quite correct, they didn't accept him in the role of a European.

One study[1] found that TV newscasters, both men and women, enjoyed a higher level of credibility when dressed conservatively in professional wear. I spoke to Annie Bishop, an Emmy Award-winning TV newscaster, who agreed with those results, but had this to add: "It's true to a point that the blazer-and-tie look can carry you a long way in the studio or in certain venues, like when you're reporting from a courtroom. But the important thing is to dress in a way that gives you credibility within the context of the story." Annie smiled. "For instance, when I was covering the Iditarod dog sled race in Alaska, I would have looked ridiculous standing ankle deep in snow wearing a business suit. I wore a big down parka and ski pants. If I were covering the Academy Awards, I'd wear an evening gown. For a National Guard training mission, I'd dress in Army camo. The key thing is that you have to look like you belong in your surroundings. It can make all the difference in how the TV audience perceives you and the trust they are willing to put in what you have to say." The point Annie makes is a good one: Be authentic.

The clothes you choose to wear each day impacts the way you feel about yourself and have an important part to play in your ability to create Three Second Windows that lead to success. When you're dressed in a way that "tells your story" and fits the setting, you're more apt to feel good about the way you look, to be more confident and more willing to put yourself forward and to interact with other people in a more positive way. When your efforts are rewarded by approval from your "audience," when you know you've passed the dopamine test, your good feelings are reinforced and you become even better at getting people on your side. You are seen as more credible, more likeable and more attractive, which means you're more likely to get the ball rolling in your direction.

Creating Symmetry, Creating Beauty

As we learned in Chapter 1, symmetry is an important part of creating an image for success. It's one of those fitness indicators we look for in the faces of others to decide whether we find them attractive. But symmetry plays a role in more than the face. There is such a thing as body symmetry, and it has a slightly different meaning than does symmetry of the face. Over thousands of years, our reward systems have developed a preference for certain body shapes that possess a kind of dynamic asymmetry that's different for women than it is for men. Our subconscious brains are able to pick out certain kinds of body symmetry—probably relating to fecundity—and release a measure of dopamine to produce the appropriate response in our neocortices. In general, it seems the ideal body shape for women is an hourglass form, while for men it's a triangle, with the wide part at the shoulders. Few of us are blessed with such perfect forms; instead, we fall somewhere between these shapes and a rectangle. Outside of body sculpting and plastic surgery, clothing is the greatest aid to creating success-oriented body symmetry. While fashions change with the seasons, the goal should be to choose clothes that get you closer to the ideal shape without compromising your authenticity. Cut, color, pattern and accessories can go a long way toward directing attention to those body characteristics that most closely approach the ideal while subtly steering the eye away from those that don't quite achieve perfection.

Over the years, I've held teaching positions in major institutions of higher learning and worked in prestigious advertising agencies. In every case, I paid special attention to how I dressed. Many of my colleagues in both the business and academic worlds took a very casual approach, wearing jeans, sneakers and T-shirts to work and even to client meetings. The rationale was that as creative people, they didn't need to worry about looking professional. The sloppy "artist" look was a signal of their disregard for social norms and so indicated a kind of creativity that set them apart from "the suits." I too dressed casually, but always projected a professional image and paid special attention to dressing in a way that emphasized the ideal masculine body symmetry of the inverted triangle. I found this approach paid off both in how my students performed and in how my clients accepted my work. In his book *Dress for Success*, John T. Molloy showed similar results in research he conducted on the subject of clothes and fashion. About his research on the effect a teacher's clothing had on the students' success, Molloy had this to say: "The outcome was that I conducted a series of experiments in Connecticut schools and proved that the clothing worn by the teachers substantially affected the work and attitude of the pupils. This was demonstrated in one case by two teachers who taught the same class in separate half-day sessions. One of the teachers wore rather casual clothing—penny loafers, a tie slightly open at the collar—while the other wore traditional lace shoes, always black, a conservative suit and a conservative tie. The students worked longer and harder for the teacher with the old-fashioned look." Molloy's work didn't prove that conservative dress always leads to success, but it did show that appropriate dress gives the wearer more validity.

There are no hard-and-fast rules for achieving body symmetry. That's because body symmetry is actually *asymmetry*. While face symmetry occurs when the left half is a mirror image of the right, body symmetry is dynamic and related more to proportion than mirror image. In women, the pleasing curve of hip, waist, breast and shoulders falls within certain ratios that vary according to overall size and height. Achieving this aesthetically pleasing relationship through the thoughtful use of clothing depends upon the individual and her ability to tap into her own reward system—to recognize the shot of dopamine she feels when she gets it just right. Men need to attune their own perceptions in the same way to find that combination of shirt, trousers, belt, shoes, socks and accessories that helps them get close to the masculine ideal of beauty. In the end, it comes down to getting in touch with your own subconscious reward system and using the pleasurable sensation it provides as a guide to discovering your own unique form of beauty and, in turn, creating your personal brand of success.

Finding Your Authentic Look

Pick up any fashion magazine and you'll find plenty of advice on style and the latest designer look. The problem is, those clothes are great on skinny models, but rarely look that good on the rest of us. Besides, fashions change from season to season and unless you've got very deep pockets, who can afford to shell out the several thousand dollars for new threads every few months? Another factor is that fashion designers design clothes that *they* like, which means their creations won't necessarily fit your own individual sense of style. So how do the average Joe and Jill develop a look that is stylish and comfortable, passes the dopamine test and is authentic? Read on.

Each of us is unique and we need to dress in a way that works for us on every level. Our clothes need to reflect our own sense of who we are. Most of us find a general look that we think is about right and stick to it throughout our adult lives. There's nothing wrong with that, but if you want to create a look that invites success, that exudes presence and personality and that gives you the confidence you need to create your own Three Second Windows, you need to let your reward system pick out your wardrobe.

You have your own body habitus, personality and self-image, and it's important to dress in a way that is true to who you are. In other words, above all else, be authentic. But what does authenticity mean in clothing? I've found that as I grow older, my taste in clothing changes. It's not an overnight transformation, it happens slowly, but it's an evolution that keeps me feeling good about my appearance while maintaining a contemporary look. My feelings about color, fabric and cut are different today than they were twenty or even five years ago, but that has very little to do with the fashion trends of the day. I check my fashion sense at the closet door and let my intuition take over. I employ the dopamine test every morning when I get dressed.

Remember the exercise earlier in this chapter when we appreciated the beauty of our hands? You can do the same thing with your clothes. The next time you go to buy an outfit, forget about what the salesperson says or those glamour shots you saw in the latest fashion magazine. Pick out an item that fits your present tastes, but also pick out something that you think *won't* work—something that's maybe the wrong color or cut or made of some fabric you wouldn't get caught dead in. Be bold and risky. Take both garments into the dressing room and try them on. Wear your safe pick first. Stand in front of the mirror and take a few slow breaths, close your eyes and clear your mind. Try to silence that voice in your head. Once you feel totally relaxed, slowly open your eyes and look at yourself. Don't focus on the new item, look at the whole you. Don't judge the new shirt or top or slacks; don't judge at all, simply notice how you feel. Are you getting that small shot of dopamine? Do you feel good about what you see? Now, perform the same exercise with the not-so-safe garment. Does it give you a thrill? Are you seeing something new in yourself? Do you feel more confident, more attractive? If so, you've found a look that is more you, more authentic than what you have been wearing. Now repeat the exercise with two or more different garments. Do a safe look and a risky look. Again, this is very important: Don't base your purchase decision on what you *think*, base it on what you *feel*. Repeat this exercise with other articles of clothing: pants, sweaters, jackets, shoes. Create combinations both risky and safe and give them the dopamine test. Try on different colors of the same shirt and see what that does. Work on refining your ability to tell which clothes and combinations of clothes produce the most pleasurable sensations. Don't think for an instant about what other people might think of your new look. Chances are excellent that if you respond positively, if your look passes your dopamine test, it will pass the tests of other's, too. Learn to recognize the shot of dopamine that's telling you you've found the basis for your new, more authentic look, one that will give you the power to create your own Three Second Windows and change those otherwise everyday moments into extraordinary opportunities for success.

Chapter 3

The Myth of the Logical Decision

Just as you need to tune into your reward system to decide what clothes to wear, it's important to learn to recognize the presence of dopamine in every other kind of Three Second Window, too. It's vital to become proficient at administering the dopamine test, because success in every sphere of your life depends on it.

We've been taught that important decisions require lengthy deliberation, that we must disregard our feelings, that all choices have to be based in pure logical thought. The fact is, nothing could be further from the truth. We have feelings for a reason; our brains have evolved to produce emotions that guide us in the right direction in every decision we make—if we know how to listen. It's true we need to temper our feelings sometimes with conscious thought, but we do that by learning how to listen to our reward systems, not tune them out. Since the Age of Enlightenment, cold, hard logic has ruled the philosophy of good decision making, but recent studies are beginning to throw those old assumptions into doubt. As early as the mid-nineteenth century, scientific evidence began to surface that pointed to the importance of emotion in the decision-making process.

The Double Tragedy of Phineas T. Gage

The accident occurred about four-thirty on the afternoon of September 13, 1848. Phineas Gage, a twenty-five-year-old railroad crew boss, was supervising the blasting when something went terribly wrong.

In order to blast the rock, Gage would drill a hole, then place a measure of blasting powder into it. An assistant would fill the rest of the hole with sand, and Gage would tamp down the sand with a long iron rod to direct the blast into the rock. On this day, Gage had just finished filling the hole with blasting powder when someone called out to him. He glanced over his shoulder for a moment, had a brief conversation, then turned back around. Incorrectly assuming the sand had been put in place, Gage began to tamp down what he thought was sand but instead was pure blasting powder. The iron rod struck a spark against the rock and the ensuing explosion went off in Gage's face, driving the iron rod through his left cheek and out the top of his head. The iron rod landed three hundred feet away.

The explosion sent Gage sprawling. Witnesses said he went into convulsions but after a few minutes sat up and spoke to them! His men picked him up, sat him in an ox cart and drove him to a nearby hotel, where a physician was summoned. Dr. Edward Williams, who responded to the call, arrived about an hour later and was astonished to find his patient sitting up in a chair on the hotel's porch, talking and perfectly rational. Dr. Edwards later wrote about that grisly moment in his rather oddly worded medical report: "He at that time was sitting in a chair upon the piazza of Mr. Adams' hotel, in Cavendish. When I drop up, he said, 'Doctor, here is business for you.' I first noticed the wound upon the head before I alighted from my carriage, the pulsations of the brain being very distinct; there was also an appearance which, before I examined the head, I could not account for: the top of the head appeared somewhat like an inverted funnel; this was owing, I discovered, to the bone being fractured about the opening for a distance of about two inches in every direction."

Amazingly, Phineas Gage recovered from his terrible accident—sort of. He showed no signs of physical disability; he could talk, move, remember and work out problems of logic as well as he did before his injury. There was one change, though: Phineas Gage had lost the ability to make good decisions.

Today, neuroscientists point to Gage's personality before and after his accident as early evidence that different parts of the brain are responsible for different functions and that emotions are crucial to the decision-making process. Before his accident, Gage was an upstanding pillar of the community. He was a conscientious employee admired by those he supervised on the railroad crew and apparently showed good judgment, high ethics and morality. In other words, he was a man of sterling character who was well known for making good, solid decisions. All that changed after his accident. Those who knew him said he'd been a shrewd businessman before his injury, but that after, he made very poor choices. Unable to hold a job, he drifted to South America, returning after a year or so to San Francisco and the care of his sister. He died in 1861, penniless and unable to support himself.

In Gage's time, little was known about how the brain works. Two competing schools of thought existed. One theorized that speech, memory, motor skills, ethics, morality—everything that makes us human and allows us to function in the world—are dispersed throughout the brain, that no one function is centered in any one part. The opposing viewpoint was that discrete mental functions are centered in discrete anatomical regions of the brain. While both schools of thought still have their proponents, it is generally accepted that the latter position is more correct. And Phineas Gage's case is a strong argument in its support.

Gage's skull has been preserved at the Harvard Medical School, and modern neuroscientists, who are able to make a pretty good estimation about what parts of Gage's brain were affected, have examined the damage and come to a conclusion. The prefrontal cortex, an important area that integrates processes from many other parts of the brain, including the areas specializing in emotion, had been badly damaged. Is it possible, then, that Gage's inability to make good decisions after his accident had a lot to do with a break in the connection between his reward system and his conscious brain? Had he lost the ability to administer the dopamine test?

Every brain has slight anatomical differences, so while it's impossible to know for sure if this is what happened to Gage's, modern brain scanning technology shows that other patients with similar personality changes exhibit damage to this same area of the brain. It would seem that people with similar disassociative conditions are unable to make good decisions. Patients who suffer from this condition tend to agonize over the simplest decisions, such as which route to drive to the local store. Is it better, they ponder, to take the shortest route, or the one with less traffic? Without the ability to connect with their feelings, without the ability to sense the presence of dopamine to guide them in a beneficial direction, they are forced to rely on conscious thought and logic only. The result is that they go adrift, unable to make good decisions or, in some cases, any decision at all. When presented with choices, they can't seem to come down on one side or the other, which makes life difficult to say the least. The problem they seem to have is that they are unable to discern an emotional preference for one choice over another.

The Wisdom of the Gut

From childhood, we're taught to make our decisions based on logic. We're told we must carefully weigh all options and make our choices only after careful deliberation and, by all means, keep emotion out of it. But contrary to what we've been told, research has shown that all decisions are actually emotional in origin. Emotion plays a key role in pointing us in the right direction. Without emotion, we are incapable of making any kind of decision at all. Our emotions provide us with an internal compass that tells us what we like, what is good for us and how to benefit from positive circumstances and avoid negative ones. Understanding how and why our emotions work is necessary to creating beneficial Three Second Windows in all aspects of life.

The conscious part of the human brain is relatively small, about the size of a table napkin and about as thick. It's very good at some tasks, such as responding to imminent threats and managing language. But it is limited in the amount of information it can handle. The bulk of the brain is made up of subconscious systems, networks and structures that are very well adapted to taking in a lot of information, sorting it out, prioritizing it and sending the important things that need immediate attention to the conscious brain.

Research has shown that the subconscious brain is better at handling very complex decisions with lots of variables, such as which car to buy, than is the conscious brain. Researchers call it decision without deliberation. Our reward systems release dopamine to help us know which choice to make. In his book *Emotional Design*, Donald A. Norman, professor of computer science and psychology at Northwestern University, has this to say about the role of emotion in decision making:

> ...Whereas emotion is said to be hot, animalistic, and irrational, cognition is cool, human, and logical. This contrast comes from a long intellectual tradition that prides itself on rational, logical reasoning. Emotions are out of place in a polite, sophisticated society. They are remnants of our animal origins, but we humans must learn to rise above them. At least, that is the perceived wisdom.... Nonsense! Emotions are inseparable from and a necessary part of cognition. Everything we do, everything we think is tinged with emotion, much of it subconscious. In turn our emotions change the way we think, and serve as constant guides to appropriate behavior, steering us away from the bad, guiding us toward the good.

Emotions are at the root of our ability to make good decisions. They allow us to make judgments about what is good for us and what is not so good. Emotions give us the reference points we need to come to well-reasoned decisions, and we rely on our reward systems to produce the proper emotions to direct us in ways that are self-beneficial. The problem lies in the fact that we've been taught to discount our feelings when it comes to decision making, so we need to practice getting back in touch with our guts and becoming familiar with the feeling produced by the presence of dopamine.

Brittney Buys a Car

Brittney is a bright, young, talented graphic designer working in a Seattle advertising agency. She has a solid design education from one of the country's finest design schools, the University of Washington, and several years of experience in the practice of design. She understands the role of the subconscious in the decision-making process, recognizes the effect of dopamine and uses that knowledge in her job every day. She also knows how to use her feelings to inform her buying decisions and choose those things that bring joy into her life and create an environment that encourages creativity and invites success. Not long ago, she was presented with a Three Second Window that turned out to make a big, positive difference in her life—all because she knew how to listen to her reward system and recognize the effect of dopamine.

During her college days, Brittney ran up considerable credit card debt and it took her a couple of years of hard work to pay it off. She swore she'd never go into debt again and for five years she held true to her oath. So when the twenty-five-year-old Toyota she was driving gave up the ghost, Brittney was determined to find a good used car and pay for it out of her savings—in keeping with her financial philosophy.

She test-drove half a dozen used cars in her price range and while she had some nagging reservations, was actually on her way to purchase one when she passed by a Scion dealership. The Scion is a neat little car based on a Toyota platform but designed specifically to appeal to the Gen-Y demographic.

Brittney hadn't even considered buying new, but one look at the new Scion and she was sold. "The minute I saw it, I knew I had to have it," she tells me. "It spoke to me in a way that none of the other cars I'd looked at did. I'd never really felt good or right about any of the used cars I test-drove. I felt like I was settling for less than what I really wanted." She shrugs. "I just had to have that little car. It made me feel good to look at it. I imagined what it would be like to own it and drive around in it." Even though buying her Scion xA meant she had to take out a considerable loan, she signed the papers without hesitation. "I still feel good about my purchase," she says. "When I went back and looked at all the factors, I think buying the Scion made a lot of financial sense…I guess down deep I knew it all along."

Brittney felt an immediate and intensely pleasurable sensation when she first saw her Scion. Her heart beat a little faster, her respiration probably sped up and it's likely that her palms became a bit sweaty. Her mind was focused on the car and all other considerations receded into the background. Her reward system was busy processing complex data and producing a positive reaction via dopamine in her conscious brain. "The car was just beautiful," she says. She was sold.

Does Brittney's car-buying experience sound familiar? It should. It resembles Jessie's experience of falling in love at first sight. The feelings Jessie felt and those that Brittney felt are similar in their origins. That's because the same physiological processes occurred in Jessie's brain when she fell in love at first sight with her guy as occurred in Brittney's brain when she fell in love at first sight with her car.

Little Love

Of course, the love we feel for other people is more profound than the love we feel for our cars. Still, the same neurostructures, chemicals and networks are involved in both kinds of love. I call them Big Love and Little Love. If Big Love is what we feel for other people, then Little Love is what we feel for things. Both are mostly subconscious and both happen very quickly. Just as we immediately know when we're attracted to another person, we immediately know when we're attracted to a thing. When Brittney saw her Scion, something about the look and feel of it triggered her reward system and her ventral tegmental area released a flood of dopamine. She instantly experienced a pleasurable sensation that her conscious brain, her neocortex, interpreted as *Hey, I like that!* And the feeling was so strong that she acted in exact opposition to her original plan to buy a used car for cash. "Well, most of the used cars I looked at had little things wrong with them," Brittney says. "They all had fairly high mileage and I knew I'd have to do a lot of maintenance on them before long. When I went back and redid the numbers, I saw that the cost of the Scion wasn't really any more than the cost of a used one, plus it fit my needs a lot better."

All her arguments make a lot of sense. Nevertheless, if it weren't for the immediate, good feeling she got from the Scion, she might have gone forward with her plan to buy a used car that in the long run probably would have been more expensive and more trouble. It was that first, brief glimpse and the feeling she got from the Scion that pointed her in the right direction. It was truly a Three Second Window.

Little Love, or the love for things, has a profound effect on our lives. We fall in Little Love at first sight with many things every day. While the emotions we experience rarely approach in intensity the rush we feel with Big Love, the result can be almost as meaningful. In a way, Brittney is married to the Scion. She'll drive her new car for at least five years—longer than some marriages last—and that's going to have a big effect on her life. It's a very small car with an engine about the size of a suitcase. Driving the Scion around is quite different from driving a bigger, more powerful car. Although the acceleration is good for a gas-sipper, she had to change her driving style. There's not much room in the car either; four people can squeeze into it but that's about all. Brittney likes to hike and garden and snow ski, and the cargo room is extremely limited. She'll have to plan her social activities and pastimes around the capabilities of her new car. But Brittney reasons that the Scion's low power and limited interior space are more than compensated for by its economy, dependability and incredible agility. The Scion corners like a sports car and parking is a dream. It's also easy on gas, so no matter how high the cost of fuel, Brittney's gas costs will be at the lower end of the scale.

Our relationships with the things that surround us—the things we use every day and that shape our lives—are intensely personal. But there's also a broader social impact associated with our possessions. For instance, Brittney's car uses little gas and oil, and its modern technology means it needs fewer tune-ups. Since the Scion is so small, fewer raw materials were consumed to manufacture it. And because her car is so compact and light, it takes up less room on the streets and does less damage to the pavement. The result is that her choice will affect us all because her small car produces fewer harmful impacts on the environment—a concern that didn't go unnoticed in Brittney's buying decision.

Savvy auto designers spend a lot of time and effort making just the right shapes and lines to successfully create attraction to and desire for their cars. They understand the power of Your Three Second Window. Brittney made her choice to buy in a few brief seconds based almost entirely on the look of the car. Though subsequent investigation and research bore out her initial impression, her quick decision process is typical of how most people make their auto-buying choices. Conventional wisdom dictates that important decisions are best made through long, logical deliberation. However at least one recent study contradicts this axiom. Researchers at the University of Amsterdam, Department of Psychology, found that car buyers who acted on their first impression made better choices than those who spent long hours consciously weighing the multitude of variables. It goes to show that we can sometimes talk ourselves out of a good choice. It turned out that "conscious decision makers" were better able to make simple decisions, while "unconscious decision makers" were better able to make more complex decisions such as those about the purchase of an automobile[1]. Researchers suggest this is because our conscious brains have less capacity to consider a large number of variables and tend to inflate the importance of some attributes over others. The subconscious, on the other hand, has a large capacity and is good at comparing and matching variables with those preferences stored, or "hardwired," in our brains. That complicated decisions are better arrived at unconsciously and simple decisions are better made at the conscious level seems counterintuitive. After all, haven't we all been taught to carefully weigh the pros and cons of every important decision? The reality, though, is just the opposite. When we learn how to trust our gut and let it inform our decisions, we usually make better choices—that is, as long as we understand the process our brains are using to make those decisions.

Even though Brittney's decision seems to have happened very quickly, her subconscious brain actually did some pretty sophisticated evaluations before signaling approval to her consciousness.

An Imaginary Conversation with Brittney's Subconscious

If we could talk with Brittney's subconscious and ask it why it chose the Scion, the conversation might go something like this:

Author: "So, what was it about the xA that drew you to it?"

Brittney's subconscious: "In a word: clarity. A car, or anything for that matter, has to be clear about what it's supposed to do. You need to be able to look at it and right away understand what it's for. If something looks really complicated, is hard to understand or has a lot of decorations on it, it probably means it's hiding some flaws."

Author: "And you felt the Scion expressed its function clearly?"

Brittney's subconscious: "Absolutely. As we were driving past the lot, I caught sight of it out of the corner of my eye. Right away, I could tell what the designers had in mind: small, quick, nimble, aerodynamic, efficient. Everything about it spoke to its function, it had a kind of honesty about it. A clarity of purpose I find very appealing."

Author: "Could you break that down for us?"

Brittney's subconscious: "Glad to. Just like when I decide if I'm attracted to another person, I look for certain things, you know, like clarity, harmony and detail."

Author: "So you actually look for those things in cars, too, before you release the dopamine?"

Brittney's subconscious: "You know it. I'm pretty particular about what I like and what I don't like. For instance, one of the first things that struck me about the Scion was its general shape. It had a certain visual harmony to it. The front end went well with the roofline, which had a nice, friendly relationship with the sides and the back. Everything fit proportionally; the windows were the right size and shape for the doors, the hood transitioned nicely into the grill and so on. You don't see that in every car. A lot of times, cars seem to be kludged together from two or three completely different models, each with a different purpose. I don't like that. It's hard to tell what the designers had in mind. I mean, we see some of these monstrosities going down the road…I don't know if it's supposed to be an SUV or a sports car, a truck or a station wagon. It's very irritating."

Author: "Hmmm. That's interesting. What else do you consider?"

Brittney's subconscious: "Well, I looked at a lot of things actually. There's a lot of little things those guys…"—Brittney's subconscious glances upward toward the neocortex and conscious brain and rolls her eyes—"just don't notice. But very little gets past me. It was my job to pay attention to the details, because they told me a lot about the Scion."

Author: "Such as?"

Brittney's subconscious: "Okay, for instance, you know the little spaces between where the doors, the hood and the trunk meet the body? Well if those little spaces aren't equal all the way around, I notice it and it bugs me. Or if there's some molding on the door and it's a little uneven or doesn't perfectly match up with the corresponding molding on the side of the car, I get really upset. It tells me that whoever built the car didn't really put much thought or care into it."

Author: "I see what you mean. But are looks really that important to the way the car performs?"

Brittney's subconscious: "Of course! If I'm not happy, no one is happy. I like things that appeal to my sense of aesthetics. If something meets my criteria and I feel good about it, then I spread the joy; if not, I can be a real nag."

Author: "So what you're saying is that the aesthetic experience is part of the car's function?"

Brittney's subconscious: "Now you're getting it."

Author: "Is there anything else about the Scion that you liked?"

Brittney's subconscious: "Yeah, see, I get bored easily. I like things that are unambiguous, sure, but I also like a little complexity in my life. The Scion has nice, clear lines, but it also has some cool little twists on the general theme. For instance, the way the headlights and taillights kind of swoop from the front and back onto the sides, almost like they are reaching out for each other. Having little visual clues like that gives me the chance to create my own interpretation and it's something I find very attractive. A definite plus."

Author: "Well, thanks for the insights. I know they keep you pretty busy around here and I appreciate you taking the time to talk with me."

Brittney's subconscious: "You're welcome. By the way, I like your eyes."

Our imaginary conversation with Brittney's subconscious, as whimsical as it may seem, gives us some insight into how our subconscious brains work when choosing things such as cars. It's a lot like the way we choose other people. I'm sure it comes as no great revelation that we tend to apply human characteristics to the objects we surround ourselves with. It's fairly common, after all, to name our automobiles, and giving ships human monikers is an age-old tradition. And who hasn't had a few choice words to hurl at a computer that insists on doing things its own way? The things we choose to include in our lives are important as much for the aesthetic pleasure they bring as for their utilitarian value. In fact, it's impossible to separate the two. One influences the other.

Things that are well designed and make us happier actually work better. When we feel good, that is, when we are being provided with a steady stream of dopamine, we tend to be more productive. Psychologist Alice Isen, a prominent Cornell University professor of psychology who studies such things, showed that people who were given a small reward before being asked to solve difficult problems that called for creativity did much better than those who received no gift at all. Even small gifts such as a piece of candy tended to increase the subject's ability to come up with fresh solutions. Isen's research shows that persons who receive a small perk and an associated shot of dopamine have more open minds and are happier, more creative, more efficient and ultimately more successful.

A Conversation with Brittney

After Brittney had driven her Scion around for a few weeks, I asked her how she likes it. "It's great," she beams. "I only spent eleven dollars for gas in the last two weeks."

"How do you like the way it drives?"

"It's like driving a sports car; it's zippy, corners really well and stops on a dime. I don't know how I ever got along with my old car."

Although Brittney had originally expressed some concern about the Scion's lack of interior space, it didn't come up once she got used to her car. Clearly the good things about her Scion so outweighed the negatives that she no longer even noticed there *were* any negatives. "Isn't there anything you'd change about it?" I asked.

She thought for a moment. "No, I think it's just about perfect."

Brittney was so adapted to the Scion that she no longer had a single negative association. This is one of the marks of a well-designed product. Brittney will drive her Scion for the next five years at least. "Buying this little car is one of the smartest things I've ever done," she says. "I wish I'd done it a long time ago."

Brittney knew that certain outward clues can give valuable information about the intrinsic goodness of a thing and used that knowledge to make a wise purchase. Designers understand how to make us feel good about the things they make because those things make them feel good, too. Their design decisions are based in emotion so that the things they make will stimulate our emotions, too.

Deconstructing Your Three Second Window

Professionals like Brittney who are trained in the design arts understand that people make their buying decisions based on emotion, then justify them with logical arguments. They know how to create things that stimulate others' reward systems, because they know how to stimulate their own. In most people, the rush provided by the release of dopamine is simply a good feeling, one they like but don't understand. The brain's reward system is about ten thousand years old and though it's adapted well to modern stimuli, it's still functioning on a pretty basic level, which means clever design can sometimes fool it into making a poor decision. Sometimes, Your Three Second Window can work against you if you don't understand it. That's why it's so important to appreciate and act upon the information your subconscious is providing, but also to realize how it works so you can make informed, wise decisions.

One of the first things I taught my design students was how to elevate a part of the subconscious to the level of consciousness. Designers have to be able to recognize that shot of dopamine and isolate the stimulus that is causing it to know when a design is right. It might be a swatch of color, a pleasing shape or an alluring texture that produces that feeling of rightness. It's not easy, but it can be done. I believe that's why art and design are so hard for some. In other professions—law, medicine, science and math—the answers are already there. It takes some problem-solving abilities and a knowledge of the discipline to reach them, but at least you don't have to invent them. Art and design are different. The solutions to art and design problems don't preexist. They are not the products of a linear thought process. The solution to every art and design problem has to be created out of whole cloth, which requires a radical departure from "conventional" thinking.

As the product of a first-class design education, Brittney was able to use her intuition—her supply of dopamine—to isolate the things that were causing her to feel good and evaluate those stimuli intelligently to make a wise buying decision. Some stimuli generated by the look and feel of the Scion were very important indicators of intrinsic quality, while a few others were simply "eye candy" and provided her with no valuable information. In fact, they might have even misled her. The general shape of the Scion was a good indicator of the thought that went into the design of the car. It revealed that the designers had spent considerable time getting the look just right, which meant they no doubt spent an equal amount of effort making it work right, too. On the other hand, there were some stimuli, such as the optional colored interior lighting that got the dopamine flowing but really didn't have anything to do with the overall fitness of the car. Brittney was able to sort out those stimuli that were important from those that weren't and apply her conscious reasoning to produce a rational decision.

Britney is a trained designer with years of experience in the practice. But, lacking her training and experience, how does the layman sort out the stimuli that are important from those that are not or, worse yet, are meant to mislead? I'll bet a lot of people's buying decisions have been heavily influenced by those irrelevant colored lights.

The next time you are in the process of making a buying decision, try this simple exercise: Isolate the various parts of the product and see how you feel about each one. I know what you're thinking—this is exactly the opposite of advice I gave on selecting a wardrobe, where I suggested you look at the whole package. But bear with me and you'll see why this makes sense.

Look at the overall shape. Disregard the color, the texture and the material and get a sense of how it makes you feel. Is there that little shot of dopamine, or does it leave you flat? If it doesn't pass this first test, chances are it's not a wise purchase for you. An unpleasant shape usually means the designers didn't spend much time on aesthetics and so they probably didn't put much effort into the rest of it either. If it does pass the shape test, next look at the fit and finish. Concentrate on the alignment of the parts. Disregard all else and get in touch with your feelings about this one aspect. What are you feeling? Is there that little thrill that tells you this is for you or are you slightly turned off? Next, give it the tactile test. Close your eyes and run your fingers lightly over the surface. Your subconscious is very good at sensing imperfections and will let you know the outcome through the presence, or lack of, dopamine.

You might find some characteristics of the product that are pleasing and provide you with that good dopamine feeling, but on reflection don't give you much in the way of information. I'm talking about what designers call ornamentation—things that are attractive, but seem added on and don't really contribute to the usefulness or aesthetic quality. Of course, each product is different and you can apply this exercise to many different aspects. By now I'm sure you get the idea. You can take this exercise as far as you want, but the important thing is to get a feel for each individual stimulus and evaluate it in relation to the whole. You will have broken Your Three Second Window down into a lot of individual, smaller ones, resulting in a more informed and wiser buying decision.

Beam Me Up, Scotty

Mountain climbers have a saying: "Good judgment comes from experience—experience comes from bad judgment." What this implies, of course, is that people have to learn the hard way, that we humans tend to trade mistakes and mishaps for wisdom. But with all we know about the human condition, it seems that there ought to be some guidelines for learning to make good decisions without going through all the pain and suffering. Could it be that recent high-technology-aided research on how the brain works can shed some light on this age-old dilemma? Could the answer be something so simple as trusting our gut feelings? It might be—with a few caveats. Studies have shown that the subconscious brain is pretty good at alerting us to potential survival opportunities and threats. It's adept at taking in a lot of information missed by the conscious brain and processing that data in a way that informs us about what course of action to take. The problem is, modern man, equipped with his penchant for cold, hard facts and pure logic, often dismisses intuition as a hindrance to good decision making. But rather than thinking of feelings as something that get in the way, new research suggests we should give emotion a greater degree of respect when it comes to deciding what's good and what's not. Of course, emotions aren't always a totally reliable guide to decision making. The drowning man who gives in to his emotions, who panics and fights the tide instead of swimming with it, will certainly do well to suppress his feelings and rely on his conscious knowledge concerning the influence of body motion on buoyancy. But without his emotional need to survive, it wouldn't make sense for him to try to stay afloat in the first place. Without the desire to live, an emotion for sure, he'd have no reason *not* to drown. So how do we know when to rely on emotion and when to rely on logic? There is a fallacy in the question that is illustrative of the central dilemma. We tend to use the word *logic* when we really mean *reason*. Logic, in its strictest definition, is confined to science, rhetoric and mathematics. Logic in this sense is void of emotion, relying solely on a set of rigid rules and equations to produce exact answers. When Spock of "Star Trek" calls some act or utterance by Captain Kirk, Bones or Scotty "illogical," what he really means is that it's irrational. Rationality can be thought of as a mix of conscious deliberation and emotional response aimed at producing a course of action that provides the individual with a survival benefit of some sort—something Mr. Spock, assuming he is coming from a strictly logical perspective, would be completely incapable of.

The story line goes that on Spock's home planet of Vulcan, the natives have evolved past the need for emotions and achieved a civilization based on pure logic. This divorce of life from feelings has produced a society without hate or war. Yet, there is an obvious contradiction in the scenario. A race of beings without emotion would not have a sense of self-preservation, since the drive to survive is emotional in its origin. This fact would make all of Spock's acts without purpose—because without feelings, he wouldn't care whether he or his fellow crewmembers lived or died—and so irrational. It would seem that Scotty's transporter beam is a more likely possibility than the existence of Spock's race of Vulcans. So we can see that we need to give credence to our feelings when making choices. The only question that remains is, how do we do it intelligently, that is, rationally?

Antonio Damasio is a professor of neuroscience, neurology and psychology at the University of Southern California and is the director of the new Brain and Creativity Institute. In his book *Descartes' Error: Emotion, Reason, and the Human Brain*, Damasio discusses both the traditional mode of decision making called "the high reason view," and his newly developed idea on decision making he calls "the somatic-marker hypothesis." According to Damasio, the traditional theory of decision making, the high reason view, proposed by such great thinkers as Descartes, Plato and Kant, assumes that "formal logic itself will, by itself, get us to the best available solution for any problem. An important aspect of the rationalist conception is that to obtain the best results, emotions must be kept *out*. Rational processing must be unencumbered by passion." This traditional view of decision making is still considered gospel by many, notwithstanding the fact that it was developed long before we were able to actually study the brain and the way it functions in real time. The high reason view of decision making involves cost/analysis reviews, extensive calculations and consideration of all possible outcomes over a period of time that could encompass one's entire life—a weighty and time-consuming effort with no guarantee of a positive result. With new developments in brain imaging technology, and concurrent evolution of thought about the anatomy and psychology of decision making, come new ideas about the best way to make good, beneficial choices, and Damasio's somatic-marker hypothesis stands out as a shining example. Basically, the somatic-marker hypothesis contends that through learning and conditioning, we develop certain emotional tags, or markers, linked to specific imagined outcomes to our decisions. It works like this: In both the high reason and somatic-marker models, we imagine a wide array of possible outcomes that could result from the choices we make. Damasio postulates that we almost never think of the present, but focus most of our thoughts on the future. And in those rare instances that we do think of the present, it's only to consider how it affects our future. We might be thinking about buying a new Mercedes and imagine tooling around town, drawing admiring stares. We might also think about how much such a luxurious car would cost and imagine working nights and weekends to make the payments. The first outcome is pleasurable, the second one not so much. Damasio, in his somatic-marker hypothesis, proposes that with each imagined outcome, there is a positive or negative feeling, and if the negative feeling is strong enough, it's a cue that our subconscious brain is telling us to avoid that outcome and to eliminate it from consideration. This process discards that possibility and allows us to focus our conscious deliberation on the remaining possible outcomes. The reverse is true, too. If we experience a positive somatic marker, it's a signal from our subconscious that the outcome is one beneficial to our well-being. Says Damasio, "Somatic markers probably increase the accuracy and efficiency of the decision process. Their absence reduces them." What Damasio is talking about is strikingly similar to the dopamine test described earlier in this book.

The Dogma Dilemma

Rush Limbaugh, the conservative radio talk show host, proclaims as part of his shtick, "I won't give up until everyone agrees with me." Limbaugh claims over twenty million faithful listeners each week, so it might be that he's well on his way to retirement. Another part of Limbaugh's act is his division of the world into conservative and liberal. He makes this distinction about everything. In Limbaugh's world, there are conservative and liberal people, conservative and liberal clothes, conservative and liberal sources of energy, conservative and liberal cars. Even conservative and liberal light bulbs! For instance, Limbaugh refuses to drive a hybrid car because it is a "liberal car." He derides wind and solar energy because they are "liberal energies," and he refuses to use low-energy compact fluorescent bulbs because they are "liberal light bulbs." Limbaugh seems to make his decisions not on the merit of the person, idea or thing, but on how he perceives its political affiliation. The reason Limbaugh gives for this bias is an overwhelming hatred for everything liberal. As part of his radio persona, he has developed such a strong emotional bias that he is blinded to the good qualities of anything or anyone he imagines does not align with his political philosophy. In his case, Damasio's somatic markers are working overtime to misdirect Limbaugh to make *wrong, harmful decisions.* In his mind, Limbaugh has created a very strong set of negative somatic markers to anything not conservative. Ironically, Limbaugh claims to eschew emotion in his decision-making process when in fact he is employing emotion in the form of his somatic markers to a larger degree than most.

We all have built-in biases that shade our thinking and decision making. Often these biases are learned through punishment or reward, and we develop knee-jerk reactions to certain words, ideas, people and constructs that prevent us from applying rationality to our gut feelings. In those cases, our feelings actually get in the way of making good decisions. We automatically dismiss some possibly advantageous outcomes simply because they have the wrong labels. This is a case where our Three Second Windows don't really get a chance to work to our advantage because they are short-circuited by our conscious biases. We cut off or ignore our dopamine and so are robbed of its value.

It's only natural for us to categorize certain people and things and place them in groups. It's an evolutionary development that has helped us survive as a species. Early humans quickly learned to place predators, poison flora and hostile neighbors into the "bad" group and to place animals that could be hunted for food, nutritious plants and friends and family members into the "good" group. Today, we still make those kinds of distinctions based on labels, and in some cases it can be a real hindrance to good decision making.

Early in the twenty-first century, America is a deeply divided nation. Roughly thirty-five percent of us self-identify as Republicans, fifty percent as Democrats and the remaining as independents. The "War on Terror" has created suspicion and distrust of Muslims and Islam among some people, and there exist two battling groups on the subject of human-caused global warming. Throw in other hot-button topics, such as a woman's right to choose, gun control and social programs like affirmative action, and we see not only an ideological divide, but an emotional chasm that is often difficult or even impossible to bridge. Could it be that we are paying too much attention to our gut feelings? Have we put too much trust in our emotional watchdogs? I think the real answer is that we simply are not using our emotions to inform our decision making in smart ways—something we are entirely capable of doing if we know the proper methods.

Let's use Limbaugh's negative somatic-marker association with hybrid cars as a thought experiment. Now, Limbaugh is a millionaire many times over, so the imagined outcome of saving money by purchasing less fuel would not apply to him. He also believes that human-caused global warming is a hoax, so the imagined outcome of emitting fewer greenhouse gases wouldn't hold up in his case, either. But he influences millions of people, and it's not unreasonable to think that there would probably be a few hundred more hybrids on the road if Limbaugh didn't take such a vocal and vicious dislike to them. So for the purpose of this discussion of decision making, let's instead use one of his listeners as an example: Joe, a self-described "ditto head" (a listener who agrees with Limbaugh ninety-nine percent of the time). Joe owns an SUV that gets nine miles to the gallon. He drives to work each day and, with rising gas prices, the cost to run his vehicle is causing a strain on his pocketbook. As Joe is filling up one day, watching the numbers on the pump spin, he imagines a future when the cost to drive to work is so high that he can no longer justify it financially. He looks from the pump to his SUV and gets a sinking feeling in his stomach. Joe's brain has just created a negative somatic-marker connection with his SUV. He's not quite as enamored with it as he was just a few minutes before. It fails his dopamine test miserably. Joe begins to idly imagine other possible future scenarios. He thinks about carpooling or even selling the gas hog and buying something that gets better mileage. He also sees himself taking the bus to work. He even imagines getting a job closer to home and riding a bicycle. All these alternatives seem to Joe to provide a better outcome than continuing to drive his SUV every day, and he begins to develop positive somatic markers for these alternative outcomes. So far, Joe's decision-making process within Your Three Second Window seems to be working just fine. Now, Joe gets into his vehicle and turns on the Limbaugh program. It's the opening monologue, and Limbaugh is talking about how snooty and superior hybrid drivers act. He describes them as effete, spineless, latte-sipping liberal snobs who hate America and everything it stands for. He describes them as unpatriotic and goes on to explain how the oil crisis and resulting high gas prices are all part of the Liberal Agenda to get us out of our big cars and into a socialist dictatorship. Limbaugh further warns that giving up our patriotic titans of the highway is tantamount to surrendering to the Liberal Environmental Wackos, with totalitarian enslavement close behind. Later in the program, he preaches against public transportation and carpool lanes as tools of oppression and part of the Liberal Conspiracy. He then draws a connection between the large number of bicycles in China and Communist World Domination.

Joe is a faithful Limbaugh listener, and he has learned over the years to attach strong negative somatic markers to those hot-button words and phrases Limbaugh is using this morning. Words such as Liberal and Environmental

Wackos, Socialist and Communist, have such strong connotations—negative somatic markers—that they overpower Joe's natural tendency to think beyond the labels, and he automatically discards any possible outcome linked to making a decision that involves them. His earlier plans to bus to work, get a hybrid car, carpool or bicycle are discarded, not because he imagines poor outcomes, but because of his strong dislike—negative somatic markers—of their labels. Something has gone terribly wrong with Joe's decision-making process.

If Joe were to get past the labels, and listen to what his subconscious reward system is trying to tell him, he might be able to envision positive outcomes associated with alternative forms of transportation. Once he did that, it would become evident that the options involving less gas and so less money are superior to maintaining the current, unsustainable status quo. But there is a desire in us all to be right. Joe has it. Limbaugh has it to a greater degree than perhaps most of us, but it's there in you and me, nonetheless. To make good decisions, we need to be able to discard the notion that we have to be right all the time and admit that we might be wrong. Taking this step frees us up to consider many more options and many more possible positive outcomes. We need to learn to listen to gut feelings and administer the dopamine test in an intelligent manner.

On Being Right

Rush Limbaugh aside, no one claims to be right all the time. If we insisted that we were right one hundred percent of the time, there'd be no room for change, no possibility of learning and no good way to make a decision, because decision making requires an internal change in the state of the mind. That's why it's so important to discard labels, biases and dogma when making choices.

When you strictly follow dogmas, political or religious philosophies or movements—what the writer, Eckhart Tolle, calls "bundles of thoughts"—you subjugate our own natural emotional compasses to the rules and regulations of others. Tolle cites the case of Cambodian dictator Pol Pot, who killed over a million of his countrymen in the service of his strict interpretation of Maoist doctrine. According to Pol Pot's reading of Mao's thoughts, anyone who wore glasses was a member of the educated class and therefore so "wrong" that he or she had to be killed. Pol Pot believed completely that he was right; he was unable to accept the possibility that he had misinterpreted Mao's teachings. His inability to discard his ideas on his dogma and listen to his true feelings about the decisions he was making led to disaster. Pol Pot believed he was in possession of Ultimate Truth and that hindered his ability to make good decisions. Many in the businesses of religion and politics claim to possess knowledge of the Ultimate Truth, and according to them, all those others who claim a conflicting Ultimate Truth are ultimately wrong.

On Being Wrong

Admitting to being wrong can be hard for some of us to do. It's only natural to want to be right, but insisting on being right all the time, even in the face of contradictory evidence, is non-productive and self-defeating. It leads to failure more often than it does to success. To make the most of each Three Second Window, you have to at least admit to the *possibility* of being wrong. Once you take that step, a whole new world opens up to you and you can use Your Three Second Windows in more positive and fruitful ways.

As we saw from the ditto-head Joe example above, our biases can pervert our naturally good decision-making processes. To get the most out of every Three Second Window, we need to turn off all our biases and preconceptions for just a moment. We have to suspend all judgment and learn to listen to our reward systems and recognize the feeling of dopamine. I can't emphasize this enough. It's possibly the most important part of learning to use our Three Second Windows to our own greatest advantage.

Try this the next time you find yourself in a sticky decision-making situation— one in which you just can't seem to make up your mind—in which all the pros and cons seem to balance each other out. Put the decision out of your mind for the time being and think about your most deeply held conviction. Maybe it's a political or religious belief. Perhaps it's a sports team affiliation. It could even be your devotion to a loved one. Now, just for a moment, discard that belief, just think to yourself, "I have no opinion or feeling about _____." You need to really be sincere, try your best to believe that you no longer hold this long-held conviction. I'm not asking you to discard the belief for good or to adopt an opposing position, just to discard it for a few moments; you can always retrieve it later. Next, work your way down the line. Get rid of as many beliefs as you can think of. Sweep your consciousness clear of biases. The purpose of this exercise is to practice suspending conscious judgment, something that often masks the dopamine and gets in the way of good decision making. Now think about the decision that's got you stuck, consider first one side and do a gut check. How does this option make you feel? Are you getting the dopamine? Perform this same exercise with the other options and compare. Does one seem to make you feel better than the others? Chances are, once you've gotten rid of your biases and let your reward system inform your decision without all the conscious clutter, you'll find the right answer and will have turned that long, drawn-out decision into a real beneficial Three Second Window.

Part Two: Your Environment for Success

Chapter 4

Designing for Success

In the first part of this book, we learned the basics of Your Three Second Window; how the reward system works, the feel of dopamine and how to use that knowledge to quickly create positive relationships with others and make better decisions. In this section, we'll explore how our environments and the things that compose them influence our lives and affect our capacities for success.

You have a lot of Three Second Windows every day. They can involve other people and the things you consider purchasing, but often they have to do with your own immediate environments. Your work and home environments have a lot to do with your ability to succeed. When you have a harmonious relationship with your environments and are living and working in comfortable, efficient space, surrounded by well-designed products, you get more done and are more creative. But it's not always immediately clear what's actually going to help shape that kind of environment and what just *looks* like it's going to help. Your spaces are complex, with lots of elements, and it can be difficult to pick out exactly which things are helping and which ones are hindering. That's because today's manufacturing processes can produce goods and furnishings that are attractive on the outside and stimulate your reward system, but are less than stellar in their performance. Manufacturers and advertisers are particularly adept at exploiting those connections between aesthetics and the pleasure and decision-making centers of our brains, so that usually you find out that a good-looking product is inferior only after you've gotten it home and lived with it for a while.

Understanding how the objects that collectively shape your environments are designed will help you spot things that have good genes, not just good looks, and ultimately will contribute to your quest for success.

Our desires to own sexy cars, big houses and beautiful clothes are all modern expressions of ancient drives. The anatomy and physiology of our brains reached their present state of evolution about ten thousand years ago, and today we apply contemporary interpretations to the survival signals being sent to our consciousness by our subconscious brains. Because we no longer are threatened by predator animals in the wild or have to forage for food or hunt game—because in modern times we don't have to evaluate the survival advantages of where we choose to live—we wind up satisfying our primitive drives in different ways: We buy things. Manufacturers and the artists and designers in their employ know how to tap into those ancient drives and get us to buy the products they make and promote—although some might consider the commercialization of artistic talent a bastardization of a God-given blessing bestowed to uplift the human spirit, not to sell microwave ovens, love seats and computers.

It's not unusual to have romantic views of artists. We might think of the starving painter living a bare existence in some lonely garret as he creates great works of the soul that will be appreciated only long after his demise. The reality is that artists and designers more often than not create their works for more utilitarian purposes. There's credible evidence that even in ancient times, long before supermarkets and department stores, the object of art and design was often blatant self-promotion and crass commercialism. Art has always been used to sell *something*: a viewpoint, a thing, an idea, a religion, a political or economic system and, yes, even the artist himself.

The Mystery of the Symmetrical Hand Axe

About two and a half million years ago, our ancestors began making cutting tools by chipping away at rocks to create sharp edges. About a million years later, *Homo erectus* figured out how to make hand axes. Archaeologists describe these hand axes as rocks that have been chipped down to about the size of a child's hand and roughly triangular in shape. Hand axes were utilitarian and used by humans all over the world. But some hand axes were clearly created not as tools but as works of art. Archaeologists know this because those axes show evidence of skill, design and aesthetics far beyond what would be required for a basic tool. Some are much too large, and some much too small, to be used as cutting tools. Many are extremely symmetrical and show no sign of ever having been used as tools.

So why did some ancient humans take the time and expend the energy to create such objects of art when basic survival required a person's total focus? In his book *As We Know It: Coming to Terms with an Evolved Mind*, Marek Kohn suggests an answer. He argues that the symmetrical hand axe "is a highly visible indicator of fitness, and so becomes a criterion of male choice." The symmetrical hand axe says something about the fitness of its creator. The man who could create such a near-perfect object demonstrated the hand-eye coordination, the strength and the stamina that are desirable in a mate and provider. Symmetrical hand axes became good indicators of strength, skill and character and were used to attract mates. In other words, they were used to sell! It seems that little has changed in all that time. Today, artists and designers still use their skills and talents to build desire into all kinds of things: cars, toasters, TVs, computers, in fact everything we surround ourselves with in our homes, businesses and modes of transportation.

Have you ever bought something that looked great but after you used it for a while, it didn't quite live up to your expectations? Maybe it was a stereo that quit working after the first year or perhaps it was a lamp with a hard-to-reach switch. It could have been something as simple as a kitchen knife that turned out to have an awkward grip. We've all made a purchase we thought was a wise choice in the store but that in everyday use turned out to be more a curse than a blessing.

On the other hand, well-designed products can make our lives better. Working on a computer with an intuitive interface makes us more productive than working with one that's complicated and awkward. A car with peppy performance is more enjoyable to drive than one with a sluggish response. A watch with an easy-to-read face is better than one with an elaborate, complicated readout. Well-designed things cause joy; poorly designed things cause misery. But is it possible to know the difference before you make your purchase and take it home? In many cases, the answer is yes.

Just as archaeologists are able to tell a lot about the purpose and usefulness of the Stone Age hand axe and about the artist who made it, you too can tell a lot about a modern, mass-produced product in the same way—but you need to know what to look for. As discussed in the first section of this book, our reward systems are very good at spotting the fitness indicators in another person that show compatible genes and a good mate. In a similar way, things, like people, also have "genes" that are revealed by fitness indicators. And our reward systems are sensitive to those as well, but with this difference: The genes of a manufactured item are not the product of millions of years of natural selection; they are the product of other people's skill and imagination. And so our reward systems can sometimes need a little help in spotting a thing's fitness indicators. That's because just as a person might disguise a blemish with makeup, a manufacturer can hide a product's poor genes with bright colors, intricate patterns or other superficial treatments. It's a lot cheaper and easier to produce a product with inferior parts, poor design and inadequate craftsmanship, then dress it up with a flashy shell, than it is to produce a truly quality item. By learning to see through such chicanery and becoming attuned to those fitness indicators that show a product's good genes, we're able to make better buying decisions and surround ourselves with things that introduce joy, not misery, into our lives.

The Bauhaus and the New Aesthetic

To know how to spot the difference between a merely attractive product and one that is both attractive and useful, it's important to understand a little of the history of mass production. Prior to the Industrial Revolution, things were made by individual craftspeople. These hand-assembled objects were conceived, designed, engineered and produced by the same person. The result was, like the symmetrical hand axe, an object with a kind of synergy that was plain to see. By the mid-eighteenth century, products began to be made in part or in whole by machine. The tasks of design, engineering and production were broken up so that no one person was entirely responsible for the finished product. The outcome was often an item that fell short in quality, usefulness, durability. It didn't take long for some manufacturers to understand that they could gain a competitive advantage by creating products that regained some of the appeal present in earlier, handcrafted products. Initial attempts to integrate aesthetics into mass production were based on mimicking the look of handmade goods. The outcome was products that simply looked like poorly produced handmade goods. They were shoddy and didn't work very well. Mass production techniques just couldn't recreate the nuances inherent in objects made entirely by the human hand. A new approach was needed.

The dawning Industrial Revolution had already made its marks on human civilization, and not all of them good. Cities swelled with the increased population of factory workers, and overcrowding in the large urban areas resulted in slums. The new industrial age posed monumental social, political, economic and aesthetic challenges. The struggle to meet those challenges would soon be taken up by a young German architect at a small arts-and-crafts school just getting started in the city of Weimar.

Architect Peter Beherns was an early practitioner of what would eventually become known as industrial design. It was 1907 when the German electric company AEG recruited Beherns to provide guidance on the mass production of its line of electric appliances, which included teapots, fans and lighting fixtures. Behrens even overhauled AEG's logo and corporate identity system. Behrens understood well the schism that existed between the practical economic necessity for modern technology and the human longing for an earlier, simpler and more spiritual time. Behrens had this to say about the conundrum:

> We need [technological benefits] today more than ever, and in the best and cheapest form. Precisely because we are economically depressed, we must make our life simpler, more practical, and more comprehensible. Only with the aid of industry can this be achieved. But those who do not want to have their life split between spirituality and technology are also right. Whether or not technology can succeed in becoming a means to and an expression of culture rather than remaining an end in itself is therefore a question of great historical importance.

A young architect named Walter Gropius was a pupil, and later a colleague, of Peter Behrens. In 1919, Gropius was appointed head of the Kuntsgewerbeschule, which he renamed the State Bauhaus. Gropius came to the Bauhaus with a reputation as a first-rate architect and forward thinker. His first major commission, a factory building, had been, as Frank Whitford writes in his book *Bauhaus,* "startlingly ahead of its time, especially in its novel use of steel and glass as substitutes for conventional load-bearing walls." The factory, built in 1911, certainly did stand out; when looking at photos of it today, it still appears modern. Gropius understood that art in the industrial age needed to take on a new, expanded role. Whitford writes of Gropius' ideas about the directions the Bauhaus should take: "The teaching programme which aimed to develop the student's personality as well as provide technical skills, were all aspects of a desire to reform not merely art education but society itself."

The Bauhaus approach was to look to processes and materials for inspiration and to shun decoration and ornamentation. Buildings were sharp and clean and geometrical. Furniture and appliances emphasized function and celebrated—instead of camouflaged—the materials they were made of and the processes that made them. The Bauhaus artists, designers and architects saw beauty in the texture of a piece of metal, in the way a stamping press formed the shape of a teapot and in the limits imposed upon them by the requirements of mass production. Before the Bauhaus, mass-produced goods were decorated to hide the processes and materials that made them. The Bauhaus approach was to celebrate those processes and materials. Bauhaus designers believed that the look of something should not only grow out of its function but its means of production, too—a well-accepted notion today, but revolutionary for its time.

The Bauhaus brought together fine artists, craftsmen and industrialists to create a new way of doing things: a mass production technique that reintegrated the tasks of conceptualization, design, engineering and production under one discipline. The result embraced and celebrated the potential of machine-made form—an approach whose results we see all around us today. Whitford writes:

> Everyone sitting on a chair with a tubular steel frame, using
> an adjustable lamp or living in a house partly or entirely
> constructed from prefabricated elements is benefiting

(or suffering) from a revolution in design largely brought
about by the Bauhaus. In the words of Wolf von Eckhardt,
the Bauhaus "created patterns and set the standards of
present-day industrial design; it helped to invent modern
architecture; it altered the look of everything from the chair
you are sitting on to the page you are reading now."

When everyday objects were conceived, designed, engineered and made by
hand, the craftsman didn't have to consider how another's production techniques
would impact his final products. But this natural relationship between aesthetics
and production was lost with the coming of the age of machine-made goods
and separation of tasks. It was left for the artists and designers of the Bauhaus
to discover new ways to reintegrate aesthetics with production techniques.
Later, other designers would apply the ideas of the Bauhaus to completely new
challenges and create completely new opportunities for success. They would
make all of our Three Second Windows even more important.

Raymond Loewy and the Coldspot Refrigerator

A 1949 cover of *Time* magazine featured a portrait of French-born industrial
designer Raymond Loewy with the headline, "He streamlines the sales curve."
Loewy understood that aesthetics sell and he used that knowledge to build a
highly successful career that spanned decades. He knew that everyday products
and appliances had to meet more than mechanical requirements; they needed
to meet the emotional, aesthetic needs of the people who used them, too. While
the essence of the Bauhaus movement was "form follows function," Loewy
believed that aesthetic appeal itself served an important economic function
by satisfying the human need to be surrounded by beautiful things. Loewy
recalled that when he first arrived in America in 1919, he was amazed "at the
chasm between the excellent quality of much of American production and its
gross appearance, clumsiness, bulk and noise. Could this be the America of
my dreams? I could not imagine how such brilliant manufacturers, scientists,
and businessmen could put up with it for so long."

Loewy started his own design studio in 1929; printed on his first business
card were these words: "Between two products equal in price, function and

quality, the better looking one will outsell the other." He knew intuitively the importance of the dopamine test and its relevance to Your Three Second Window. Loewy proved this maxim time and time again with successful, modern-looking products. One such success was the refrigerator he created for Sears, Roebuck and Company in 1934. Loewy had this to say about redesigning the Coldspot:

> When we began our design, the Coldspot unit then on the market was ugly. It was an ill-proportioned vertical shoebox "decorated" with a maze of moldings, panels, etc., perched on spindly legs high off the ground, and the latch was a pitiful piece of cheap hardware; we solved these problems in no time. The open space under the refrigerator was incorporated into the design and became a storage compartment. The new latch was substantial as well as attractive (like the door of an expensive automobile), the hinges were made unobtrusive, and the name plate looked like a piece of jewelry. The new design connoted quality and simplicity.

In advertisements for the Coldspot, Sears invited potential customers to "study its beauty." To consumers, the look of the appliance must have been as important as its function, because the Coldspot refrigerator was an instant success, quadrupling sales of previous models. Loewy went on to have a hand in creating many icons that are fixtures of the American psyche: the Greyhound bus, the Avanti automobile and Air Force One, to name just a few. He even contributed to the work done by NASA, including Skylab and the space shuttle.

While Loewy's designs always appealed to the aesthetic senses, he never overlooked the other principles governing the creation of well-designed things. He understood the production techniques and designed his products to be easy and inexpensive to manufacture. Loewy also knew that the objects he made had to be usable. He made sure that people would be able to understand his products' functions and how to use them. He believed that the things that shape our everyday lives have to be easy and economical to maintain. Loewy understood that good design is more than just good looks—that in order for a manufactured object to be truly useful and contribute to an environment that invites success, it must work on a utilitarian as well as an aesthetic level. Once you've learned to recognize the feeling of dopamine, you can judge whether something is going to contribute to the aesthetic quality of your environment. But even a beautiful product will eventually seem ugly if it doesn't work very well, if it introduces misery instead of joy into your life.

We might get the intuitive dopamine rush from a beautifully designed product, but it takes some conscious understanding of the different kinds of design to judge whether a manufactured product is going to perform as well as its appearance suggests. Sometimes our reward systems need a little help from our consciousness to make the most of every Three Second Window.

Your Three Second Window and the Three Kinds of Design

In his book *Emotional Design*, Donald A. Norman discusses the three kinds of industrial design: visceral, behavioral and reflective.

Visceral Design

Visceral Design, Norman says, "is what nature does." Visceral design is the most basic, intuitive type. It appeals directly to our subconscious brains and is the kind of design most responsible for creating initial attraction in things. The appeal of visceral design is related to the look and feel of an object, whether it is a car, a computer, a house or a carving knife. When we respond to visceral design, we are feeling that shot of dopamine that tells us our human needs are being met. This kind of design engages our reward systems directly and so might be the most powerful of the three. Our attraction to visceral design is hardwired; it's the result of millions of years of evolution and it's what draws us to a product in the first place. Over the millennia, we have developed certain preferences for shapes, color combinations, textures, sounds, scale and proportions, and when these principles are skillfully incorporated into everyday objects, we are immediately drawn to them. Ultimately, they go a long way toward enhancing our lives and making us more successful. They are the initial dopamine triggers and hold powerful sway in Your Three Second Window.

Behavioral Design

Behavioral design is based on how things are used by people. The heft and balance of a hand tool; the knobs, switches and readouts on a stereo; the handling, seating comfort and fuel economy of an automobile—all are considerations falling under the heading of behavioral design. When designers think about how something will be used, they are thinking about human behavior. Good design takes this into account from inception, but often things are made without thinking about who will use them or how they'll be used. Things designed and manufactured in this way are more a hindrance to success than a help.

I once had a client, a large electronics manufacturing company, that made all kinds of high-end testing tools for engineers. Part of my job was to visit with the engineers and have them explain to me how the gadget they had designed worked. It was my task to convert the technical lingo into an ad that would appeal to a certain target audience. I had to create attraction for things that weren't intrinsically attractive. At the time, a philosophy of "designing for the next bench" was in vogue. Engineers would design tools for the engineer at the next bench or cubicle—in essence, for themselves. They built them just because they could. I remember asking the engineers, "Is there a demand for this gadget?"

The reply inevitably would be, after some hesitation, "People don't know they need it…but if they did, they'd want it." Most of these inventions never saw the light of day, and although a few met with grudging acceptance, none was ever what could be called a roaring success. The problem was that these engineers didn't take into account behavioral design principles. Instead of creating something to fill a demand, they created a product hoping the demand would magically spring into being. Had they known of and followed Loewy's axiom—MAYA: Most Advanced, Yet Acceptable—their designs would have met with much greater acceptance and success.

The first criterion for good behavioral design is function. Does the thing do what it's supposed to do and how well does it do it? The next key to good behavioral design, Norman says, is understanding. Norman puts it this way: "After function comes understanding. If you can't understand a product, you can't use it—at least not very well. Oh, sure, you could memorize the basic operating steps, but you probably will have to be reminded over and over again what they are. With a good understanding, once an operation is explained, you are apt to say, 'Oh, yes, I see,' and from then on require no further explanation or reminding. 'Learn once, remember forever' ought to be the design mantra."

Feedback is, according to Norman, another important part of understanding. Interaction between humans and machines requires input from the person and output from the machine. The machine in this way becomes an extension of the person using it. How well that thing serves this function has a lot to do with good two-way communication. Often we think of our interaction with a machine as simply telling it what to do and having it do it. But in reality, there's a lot more to it than that. The machine has to communicate back to us; it has to let us know that it has received our instructions, that it can perform the required task—or why it can't—and where it is in the process of completing the task. Examples of feedback are the vibration transmitted from the road through the steering wheel of your car and the bite of a snow ski's edge as you transfer your weight. Inadequate feedback is a source of frustration. Think how you feel when the little clock just spins and spins during some long computer operation or, worse yet, freezes up entirely with no explanation why. Good behavioral design, Norman insists, is built into the product from inception. It can't be added on at some later point in the process. You can make some judgments about the visceral design of a product just by looking at it, but to know if it possesses good behavioral design, you have to be able to touch and feel the thing. How it rests in the hand, how the controls behave, the texture of the materials and its heft and balance are all attributes designers call tangibility, and they have to be experienced firsthand. A photo or an image on a computer screen just doesn't give you the kind of sensual input necessary.

Reflective Design

Reflective design is the most esoteric of the three kinds. It relates to the image a thing conveys. For instance, a Rolex watch projects an image of wealth and taste. It probably doesn't tell time any better than a Timex, but it certainly sends a different message about the person wearing it. The Timex also sends a message. It might be that the wearer isn't concerned with being flashy, but is more interested in practical matters. In both cases, reflective design plays an important role.

Reflective design relies heavily on culture, time and fashion. A 1957 Cadillac convertible sends a much different message today than it did in the year of its manufacture. In '57, such a car would speak to affluence, style and a concern with having the latest and the greatest. Today, that same automobile might reflect the owner's sense of nostalgia, humor or interest in old cars. Conversely, the brand-new Caddy would have had still different meanings in different cultures. In a third-world country in 1957, the car might have reflected American imperialism, while at Monte Carlo it could have sent the message that the owner is an accepted member of the upper crust.

Understanding the thinking and the processes that go into the conception, design, engineering and manufacture of mass-produced goods gives you insight into what constitutes good design and helps you make better buying decisions. Visceral, behavioral and reflective design all have their roles in creating objects that will enhance your daily life and help you create an environment that invites success. While each kind of design assumes a different level of importance depending on a given product's purpose and an individual's reasons for acquiring it, careful evaluation on all three levels will help you assess the role attraction plays in your buying decisions and help ensure you select the best product for your needs.

Dopamine and the reward system provide us with an emotional compass and help us choose those things that will enrich our lives. In a simpler time, we could rely solely on the outward appearance of a thing to judge its quality. Today, when choosing manufactured goods, we need to look deeper and employ our intellect, but we can still depend on our reward systems to provide invaluable guidance—if we know how.

Looking Deeper

If you've read this far and practiced the exercises, you've no doubt begun to recognize the release of dopamine by your reward system—and you've got a good start on creating an environment that invites success. Try this exercise to help create harmony in your home or office: Look around and pick out a manufactured item. The simpler the better: a stapler, a pencil sharpener, a ballpoint pen. Quiet your thoughts. Now isolate each of the levels of design. Look at the thing from a purely visceral perspective. Without picking it up or touching it, try to perceive how its appearance makes you feel. Give it the dopamine test. Look at all the visual components one at a time: the shape, the color, the fit of the various parts. Can you feel the dopamine? Next, pick up the object. Close your eyes so that you can eliminate the visceral cues and focus only on its behavioral qualities. How does it feel in your hand? Is it well balanced, is the texture pleasing? Run your fingers over the entire surface and see how that makes you feel. Work its controls. Does it respond immediately? Are the actions sharp and clean or delayed and sloppy? Do you get a sense that it is performing its requested task? Remember, you're looking for that little spark of joy that indicates the release of dopamine. Now let's evaluate its reflective qualities. Place the object in its intended environment, perhaps on your desk or a shelf; a pen in your pocket or a desk holder. Get a sense of how it impacts the other things around it. Does it make your desk look cheap in comparison or vice-versa? Is the pen elegant and projects class or is it utilitarian and conveys practicality? How does each of these impressions make you feel? Now consider the object in its entirety and do a gut check. Can you tell whether it brings harmony or chaos to your environment? What is your reward system telling you? What is the result of this Three Second Window? You can go through your home or office and perform this exercise on other manufactured products, too. You'll quickly identify those things that bring joy into your life that help you build a more harmonious and creative relationship with your surroundings and create an environment that invites success every moment of every day!

The Nature of Space

A few summers ago, my three daughters and I took a trip to Europe. One of our first stops was Notre Dame Cathedral in Paris. I had visited the cathedral before, but it was a first for my children. As we entered and strolled into the nave, my gaze wandered to the ceiling far above and I was suddenly overcome by a sense of vast space. I remembered having the same feeling the first time I was inside Notre Dame, several years before, and it was no less profound this time. Notre Dame, like the other cathedrals of Europe, is made of stone, but the large clerestory windows high above and the verticality of the columns give Notre Dame a sense of height and lightness. Looking up into the ceiling, you can almost "see" the space. "It's like looking into heaven," as I overheard one tourist say. The feeling is immediate and overwhelming and, without realizing it, I stopped in my tracks and stood transfixed, drinking in the airiness and light. I turned to my girls, and they, too, stood staring up at the ceiling, faint smiles on their faces. It was a medieval Three Second Window!

We don't normally think of space as something made or manufactured, but in fact it is. The room or patio, park or office, bus or train you are sitting in right now consists of man-made space. And the nature of that space has a profound effect on how you feel. Sometimes it's immediately overpowering as in Notre Dame, but more often it is subtle, and its effect on our moods is less obvious—but there, nonetheless. Some spaces feel cozy and comforting, others convey a sense of greatness and power. Some spaces—government buildings, for instance—can make us feel small and insignificant. Many times buildings such as libraries and commercial properties are designed to produce a welcoming effect. Some buildings create space on a human scale, others on a monumental scale. Each has its impact and each has its purpose. Creating space and controlling the effect it exerts on people is an art developed over the history of humankind. Today, the design of space is mainly the job of the architect, and architecture has become formalized into styles, periods and idioms.

But in the beginning, shelter was something common people sought out in the natural landscape. We were wanderers then, hunter-gatherers following the migration of game, seeking refuge in caves and rock overhangs from the ravages of wind, rain and cold. These were the places nature provided for protection from the elements, and early man's survival depended upon locating them. Life would have been tenuous; a failure to find natural shelter could mean remaining outside in appalling conditions—it could even spell doom for the whole group. Perhaps it was this basic instinct for survival, or maybe an evolution of thought about natural forms, that inspired the first human to come up with the idea of creating an artificial cave: a man-made structure that provided shelter from the elements. Whatever the source of inspiration, that first building would be a pivotal event in the development of civilization. It would represent the first man-made space. It would mark the invention of architecture.

Stone Age humans sought out environments that provided secure and bountiful places to live. Our hardwired preference, developed over thousands of years, is for characteristics of land, flora and fauna that give us our best shot at continued survival. Today, we no longer have to be as particular about *where* we live. Civilization has given us the ability to create desirable environments just about anywhere we want. Still, we exhibit the same primitive preferences for form and space—developed in the dim past—when we design a room or build a house, a shopping mall, a skyscraper or an entire city.

Some of the earliest examples of man-made shelter are found at Terra Amata, a site near modern-day Nice in France. The Terra Amata shelters date back to a very early period in human development, around 450,000 B.C. The site contains the remains of circles of stones that archaeologists think anchored sticks and branches used to form shelters with cave-like arched walls and ceilings. Inside, these shelters must have been very similar to the inside of a natural cave or rock overhang.

What muse guided the hands of these ancient builders as they created shelters similar to caves? Was it a conscious effort to copy a form they were already comfortable with?

Perhaps they were inspired by the materials available to them. Or maybe they were simply driven by their hardwired preferences for one particular type of space over another. Is it possible that their reward systems were telling them, through dopamine, how to build a structure that would help them survive? While the answers to these questions will probably never be known for certain, later archaeological evidence sheds some light on what inspired ancient builders.

Inspiration for Success

Terra Amata was a small village temporarily used by roaming hunters on a seasonal basis and, in its own way, represented a successful leap of the imagination. Remains of one of the earliest known *permanent* settlements have been found in modern-day Turkey in an area known as Anatolia.

Catal Huyuk dates back to the Neolithic period, or New Stone Age, of about 6,000 B.C. It appears builders at Catal Huyuk had abandoned the cave-like structures of Terra Amata by this time and begun constructing settlements devoid of visual reference to natural shelters. The builders at Terra Amata built directly with raw materials they could readily find: stones, sticks and branches. In contrast, the Catal Huyuk builders used raw materials to *manufacture* structural elements such as clay bricks and wooden beams. This is one of the first settlements where the structures are completely abstract; that is, they do not in any way mimic the appearance of natural shelters. They do, though, recreate the sheltering function of caves the same way the shelters at Terra Amata did. The Catal Huyuk dwellings were, in fact, abstract caves. The clay bricks took the place of living stone. What inspired these Neolithic builders to build the way they did? Did they experience many Three Second Windows that guided them in the right direction? Did they, in their own ways, administer dopamine tests to determine suitable forms? Since they apparently abandoned any literal reference to older forms, they must have found their inspiration in other places, in other ways.

Catal Huyuk is near the Carsamba River on a great fertile plain, the remains of an ancient lakebed. As the lake dried, about sixteen thousand years ago, many smaller lakes and swamps remained. This made it an ideal place for animals to gather, so that the people of Catal Huyuk didn't need to roam to hunt, and the alluvial soil provided abundant crops. Because of the ample food supply, this region was a perfect place to erect a permanent settlement. But building materials that could be used in their raw form were scarce. There were few stones, so these Neolithic builders were forced to create *abstract* stones out of clay. While not resembling natural stone in appearance, the bricks served the same purpose, but much more efficiently. By creating uniform bricks, the New Stone Age builders were able to take an even further leap of abstraction. Instead of building shelters that looked like caves, they could now build shelters that performed the function of caves but took on a different form—one that lent itself to the manufacturing process. The homes, shrines and shops at Catal Huyuk were rectangular in shape and connected to each other in much the same way units in modern apartment complexes and shopping malls are.

Sometimes inspiration comes from the environment, as it did at Terra Amata, and sometimes it comes from introspection, as it seems to have at Catal Huyuk. The right angles and rectangles found in the box-shaped buildings at Catal Huyuk do not exist in nature. So it seems that while the builders at Catal Huyuk took few cues from what nature had to offer, they certainly were inspired by what nature *failed* to provide. In the absence of natural building materials that could be used in their found state, the Catal Huyuk builders looked inside themselves for the inspiration to create new abstract forms, not only in the individual structural elements, but in the shape of the actual buildings themselves. The interiors show a remarkable attention to scale, proportion and detail, creating comfortable spaces that—with the addition of plumbing and power—would be livable even today. It's fascinating to think about the process the first Catal Huyuk builder must have gone through to come up with the idea for an abstract cave. He would have had little to go on, certainly no example to copy. He must have had a very active imagination to see bricks in the clay and cities on the plains.

From Spectator to Participant

From the outside, you experience architecture as something to be seen. Once inside, the experience changes drastically; you become a part of the design and participate in the life of the building itself. As important as good design is to the exterior, the interior space can have a much greater effect on how you feel. Frank Lloyd Wright, arguably the greatest architect of the twentieth century, said, "The interior space itself is the reality of the building." Wright, like all great designers, understood the importance of interiors and the role they play in creating environments that can nurture success.

When you look at the outside of a building, you have a Three Second Window in which you get a feeling for what kinds of activities go on inside. If it's a chrome and glass skyscraper, you know there will be offices inside. A rustic log and stone structure suggests cozy rooms for sleeping and eating. A tidy craftsman-style bungalow is someone's cherished home. Whatever the purpose, the exterior sets up certain expectations for the interior, expectations that when satisfied help set the stage for your reward system to give you that shot of dopamine.

Wright believed that cohesiveness was an important principle not only in the outward appearance of a building, but in the relationship between the exterior and interior. He established visual themes for his projects that ran throughout, from the height of the walls and the slope of the roof to, in some cases, the furniture, carpets and silverware. It's said that Wright even designed his wife's clothing to fit with his architectural designs. Wright created spaces that people could interact with on a human scale, and no detail was too small for consideration—he understood the Three Second Window and how good the human eye is at sizing up an entire room in a single glance. Though you may not consciously notice those details that are a little "off," your subconscious immediately registers the discrepancies and notes that something isn't quite correct. On the flip side, when care and attention have been given to the design and arrangement of a room, and the designer has gotten it just right, your reward system is triggered and you get the feeling that *this is a place I want to spend time in.*

Wright was a transcendentalist with a deep and abiding love and respect for nature and the way people relate to it. Bruce Brooks Pfeiffer writes in his book *Wright:*

> Frank Lloyd Wright regarded nature in almost mystical terms. He deeply believed that the closer man associated himself with nature, the greater his personal, spiritual, and even physical wellbeing grew and expanded as a direct result of that association. Wright liked to refer to his way of thinking of nature as "Nature spelled with a capital 'N' the way you spell God with a capital 'G'," and he further maintained that "Nature is all the body of God we will ever know." From this point of view, from his reverence and subsequently his respect for nature, his buildings, where placed in the landscape, had this one aim in common: to let the human being experience and participate in the joys and wonderment of natural beauty.

Wright's feeling about the beauty of nature is evident in his interior designs. Just as nature leaves nothing to chance, Wright also paid special attention to every detail that could have an impact on the interior feel of his buildings: the lay of the land, the rising and setting of the sun, the prevailing wind patterns and predominant weather conditions. Considering Wright's passion for nature, it's no surprise that natural light was important to him and played a key role in his designs. His interiors employed an open plan that eliminated many partitions and doors and replaced them with architectural elements to divide the space. Walls were no longer walls, but "screens" and windows no longer holes, but "openings in screens." This approach allowed more sun to enter the rooms and helped celebrate the play of light and shadow to the benefit of human enjoyment and comfort.

Light and Color

Anyone who has ever been in a Wright house will tell of a distinct feeling upon entering. It's one of space and light and a sense of welcoming. The attention to detail invites a more intimate involvement with the house. A Wright house is not only a work of art, but a place you'd want to live.

Light and color are critical elements in Wright's design of interior spaces. He understood the need for adequate illumination for everyday tasks such as cooking, bathing and navigating at night, but he knew there is another function of light just as important, and that is its effect on the way we feel. In his book *Color and Human Response,* Faber Birren talks about the psychological and physical effects of light on humans. He quotes Dr. Thomas R.C. Sisson, of Rutgers Medical School, who writes, "Light does not merely lend illumination to human existence but exerts a powerful physical force, affecting many compounds within the body, some metabolic processes, the life and generation of cells—even the rhythms of life. Light is ubiquitous, it can be manipulated, and it is not entirely benign."

It's not surprising that light is necessary for our physical well-being. What is interesting is that light enters your body not only through your eyes, but through your skin, muscle and even bone! In fact, some studies suggest that light entering through the skull activates photoelectric cells in our brains and affects our moods. An experiment conducted by E.E. Brunt found "that light does reach the temporal lobes and hypothalamus in a variety of mammalian species." Birren elaborates on Brunt's findings: "This means that light is essential to a healthful and normal life and that nature has evolved ways in which it affects your body through the tissue of your skin, your eyes, and even your skull itself."

As the sun moves across the sky, the amount and quality of light that enters a space change and these changes are reflected not only in terms of candlepower and wavelength, but in your mood, too. It turns out that these light and dark rhythms have a big impact on your physiological and emotional states. When the light changes, so does your blood pressure and body temperature, and even some hormone secretion is affected. Light not only affects you physically, but it also affects the way you experience the spaces you occupy. For instance, different light sources, even natural light at different times of day and in different weather conditions, change the way colors look. Natural daylight contains all the colors of the rainbow, and colors seen in daylight tend to look richer and more deeply saturated. Other types of artificial lighting can run the spectrum from cold blue to warm yellow and red, causing the things they illuminate to take on different hues. This variance in the appearance of color due to different light conditions is so important that at our agency, we have a special light booth with controlled wavelength illumination so that we can judge colors in a standard light.

Creating harmony with your surroundings is essential to creating space that invites success. Color and light play a vital role in creating harmony, so it's important to understand the relationship between these two elements. Color and light are inseparable. You can't have one without the other. When you enter a dark room, what do you see? It's not until you introduce light that color becomes visible. Think about the space you're in right now and consider the way the light is affecting the color of the walls, the floor, the window coverings, furniture, objects and photos or art that may be present. The effects of light reflecting off these areas are what—when combined—create either a comfortable, encouraging environment—that is conducive to creativity and so welcomes success or an environment that lacks these qualities. A Three Second Window exercise that helps create that kind of welcoming space is to sit in a comfortable place in the room. Look straight ahead, but notice what you're seeing out of your peripheral vision. Is there anything that grabs your attention? Perhaps it's the way the light from a lamp reflects off a wall. Is it a pleasing distraction, one that provides a little release of dopamine, or is it bothersome? Try changing the direction or placement of the light. Now look at it again out of the corner of your eye. What is your reward system telling you? You can turn the light off altogether or change the type and wattage of the bulb and repeat the exercise. What kind of feeling do you get? Sit or stand in various places in your room and try this exercise again. Eliminate those light/color interactions you find objectionable. You'll be amazed at how much more comfortable, calm and creative you become.

I spoke with Susan Thomas, who is a principal in Clear, a company that stages homes for the real estate industry. Her job is to make houses appeal to potential buyers by creating interiors that make the prospects feel at home "from the minute they walk in the door." I asked Susan about the role light plays in making a house welcoming from the get-go. "The minute someone walks into one of our homes," Susan says, "I want them to feel like they belong there. Every room has a story to tell, and the first story told should be 'welcome home'."

Susan continues, "I really use light to make that happen. I use a lot of light, I turn on every lamp, but I make sure there are shadows, too, because it gives the room a sense of depth. I also use light to direct the potential buyer's attention to a focal spot in the room, one feature, like a fireplace or a sculpture or a painting, that sets the mood for what is to come. I like incandescent light, no fluorescents, because the incandescents have a nice, warm yellow glow, and that says home to just about everyone."

When I asked Susan about the role of color in creating a nurturing environment, she thought a moment. "There are so many variables when it comes to color; the size of the rooms, the kind of light, windows, and of course personal taste are all factors so that you have to take each place on its own terms. Generally, though, if I had to say, I'd say warm primary colors are preferable to the cooler colors and colors that are mixtures of the primary colors."

Studies about color preference bear out what Susan had to say. And our preferences for colors change over our lifetimes. While it's impossible to predict what any one individual's favorite colors are, color preferences have been rated over large groups, so that researchers can say generally what colors *most* people like best. It appears that infants prefer the luminous colors: Yellow, white, pink and red are the colors they seem to stare at the longest when tested. As we get older, we seem to prefer yellow less and blue and red more. As we mature, it appears our preferences change again, and we begin to like the blues and greens more. In numerous studies conducted over the years, such as one by research psychologist H. J. Eysenck involving more than two thousand people, the results have been about the same. Adults overwhelming prefer blue, followed closely by red, green, violet, orange and yellow. This ranking of color preference holds true across sexes and cultures.

While color and light play important roles in creating attraction and desire for potential home buyers, I was interested in what Susan thinks is the biggest influencer. "It's no one thing," she says, "it's the total effect. You have to get the feel of the house, then arrange the furniture, direct the lighting, apply the colors and create textures that highlight the best features of the home and make potential buyers feel as though they could walk right in and set up housekeeping. One thing that is extra important to making a house feel like home is to create soft surfaces: drapes, pillows, interesting fabrics and so on. The colors, textures and patterns of the fabrics, little things like that, have a huge impact on the overall feeling you get when you first step into a room."

Jean Orlebeke is a graphic designer who works from her studio in the hills of Oakland, California. She designs the patterns you see in fabrics used on the walls of office cubicles, in hotel lobbies, on airplane bulkheads and seats, for pillows, bedding, you name it. Her patterns are used in Herman Miller furniture and by other upscale furniture manufacturers. She also designs wrapping paper and wallpaper. Her amazing geometric patterns are a real treat to the eye, and I asked her how she comes up with them. "I start with a single element," she says, "some little interesting detail that is pleasing to the eye, then work on a system for repeating and elaborating on that theme." Jean designs patterns for home and for the commercial environment. I asked her if she approaches each use differently. "Absolutely," she says. "When I'm doing something for a commercial interior like an office, the pattern needs to be a bit more muted. I might design a pattern to go on a wall that has a bright focal point, but I'd treat the cubicle walls somewhat differently, a bit more subdued."

What about the home environment? "Oh, I think that's about the most fun you can have. You can go really wild and come up with some very stimulating patterns because it doesn't have to please a general audience, you can design things you like and hopefully, some homeowners will like them too. But whether it's for commercial or residential, it all starts with that one little element that gets repeated over and over—translated and retranslated. How you manage the spaces and the colors and the minutiae really makes the overall pattern work."

Alas, very few of us can live or work in a building designed by Frank Lloyd Wright or staged by Susan Thomas or with fabrics by Jean Orlebeke. We can, however, benefit from their ideas about attention to detail and the important role it plays in creating environments that trigger the release of dopamine and make for spaces that invite success. All are talented designers whose work is very much in touch with their own sense of rightness.

Feng Shui

In recent years, the ancient Chinese practice of feng shui has begun to catch on in the West. Its practitioners claim that feng shui can have a big, positive influence on your success both at home and in your work. Feng shui is the art of achieving balance in life, encompassing the landscape, the house and the home's interior space. In the West, we think of a thing as either living or inanimate: A person is a living being, a house is not. Feng shui does not make this distinction. To the feng shui practitioner, all things are imbued with a basic life force called ch'i. Sarah Rossbach, in her book *Interior Design with Feng Shui*, says of ch'i: "Out of the interaction—balancing and harmonizing—of the forces of yin and yang arises the theory of ch'i—meaning both cosmic breath and human energy or spirit."

The proper flow of ch'i throughout the home is the goal of feng shui. It is believed that ch'i not only affects how you feel in your home, but also influences your finances, your relationships with others and your health. For instance, blocked ch'i can lead to stagnation in a relationship, while a direct flow of ch'i from the front door to the back door can cause money to flow out as fast as it comes in. Rossbach writes: "Home ch'i can also affect our personal ch'i. The study of environmental ch'i is an important part of feng shui. For instance, if your entrance door opens onto a wall, then your ch'i will be blocked. Having to move around the wall as soon as you enter will affect your posture, and coming up against the wall will make you feel defeated, lowering your expectations in life. As a result, you will struggle."

Feng shui is detail-oriented, paying attention to every aspect of a room's construction, the arrangement of furniture and placement of plants and mirrors, as well as the color scheme. Feng shui practitioners have been advising on the interior design of commercial establishments and private homes in China for centuries and in the West for several decades. As a result, many Westerners who have used feng shui report a dramatic improvement not only in the quality of their living and working spaces, but in their emotional and financial situations—even in their relationships with others.

Although the principles of feng shui are Chinese in origin, they seem to jibe with many Western concepts of interior design. In a lot of ways, they're not that different from the philosophy behind Wright's work: open space, flow and attention to detail. The fact that ancient Eastern and modern Western concepts about design can produce similar effects in our reward systems suggests that all humans share the same basic aesthetic preferences. Feng shui is based in spirituality, while Western design relies more on practicality as its foundation. It's fascinating to ponder, though, that both philosophies tend to generate the same human emotional response: the production of dopamine by our reward systems.

The principles of design—scale, balance, visual rhythm, harmony, proportion and emphasis—have been important in all great architecture in both Western and Eastern cultures. When all these principles are applied with competence, we find the resulting space to be satisfying. We feel secure and welcome and experience a sense of belonging, which makes success much more attainable. Our reward systems recognize certain fitness indicators and we are given that shot of dopamine that tells us *this is a space that will help me succeed.*

We get used to the feeling of our own homes and workplaces. We like to sit in certain spots, develop our own patterns of movement and arrange lighting to meet our needs. Our environments change and evolve over time as we try out new arrangements. Much of the way our environments look and feel is the result of necessity: The couch has to go where it won't block access to the bedroom door or the plant has to be next to the window to get enough daylight. Too often, we create spaces that work on a purely mechanical basis, but fall short of meeting our emotional needs. Usually this happens because we fail to pay attention to the details. If we think about emotional needs as an important part of function, suddenly the opportunities to create a welcoming space and a sense of belonging become apparent.

Try this simple exercise. You'll be amazed at what you see:

Go outside, walk up to your front door and create a Three Second Window. Pause a moment and do a dopamine test. What do you feel? Does your entrance have a human scale? Does the opening feel too high or too low? Too wide or too narrow? Is it inviting or unpleasant? Open the door and move just inside. Try to isolate that experience of transition between the outside and inside. Step back through the threshold and repeat the experience. Does your feeling change as your environment changes? Is it better or worse? Once inside, does the space have a satisfying feeling of balance or do you feel too confined or too exposed? Is there a pleasing rhythm of shapes, sizes, colors and furniture arrangement? Pick out those things that give you a pleasing shot of dopamine and work on emphasizing them through the use of light and color or the arrangement of objects such as plants, sculpture or screens.

Now that you're inside your house, do you get a feeling of belonging? Is there a harmonious relationship between the room's elements that results in a pleasing sense of wholeness? When you move through the space, do the furniture and pictures on the walls relate to the room in a pleasing, proportional way? Do some things feel too big for the room or too small? As you look around your room, do you notice a focal point, something interesting or an area of emphasis that draws your eye and sets the mood for the whole room? Try to "feel" the space. Turn off the TV and the stereo. Stand and sit in different places, contemplate the feeling each part of your space evokes.

Short of a major remodel, there's little you can do about the actual placement and proportion of doors and windows, but you can easily alter how they make you feel through the use of color, light, pattern, window treatments, furniture and object placement. Experiment with color swatches and cardboard cut-outs that simulate real things such as furniture, lamps, and wall hangings. Isolate the different design elements, check how the different space shapes make you feel. Perform a dopamine test on various arrangements and combinations. You'll discover that where you place things and how you deal with color and light have effects almost as profound as actually moving walls and reshaping doors and windows.

Objects such as sofas have their own shapes, but also shape the space around them and impact how we perceive and feel that space. Moving a piece of furniture a few inches can change drastically the sense we get from a given space. See how you feel about how the furniture relates to the windows and doors, and not just from a purely mechanical perspective. Tune in to the emotional effect, too. Does the space created around a chair complement or conflict with the space created around a nearby floor lamp or photo hanging on the wall? These might sound like esoteric considerations, but they really do have a big impact on how livable your space is. Once you learn to see and feel space, you'll be able to create environments that are more enjoyable to inhabit, help ensure a steady flow of dopamine and invite success.

By evaluating your home through the language of design, you should begin to see where it works and where improvement is needed. In other words, you are designing your space to invite success, just like Frank Lloyd Wright.

Chapter 5

Impulse Nation

As you work to create your harmonious environments, you will eliminate some things and replace them with others. You will experiment with light and color, add and subtract and rearrange until you get it just right. You will aim for a space that stimulates the regular release of dopamine and helps you be more creative and more successful. But as you venture forth into the marketplace to choose those things that will contribute to a harmonious environment, you are entering a dangerous place indeed—one where marketers try to manipulate your reward system to get you to buy their wares. They'll use every trick in the book to manipulate those connections between aesthetics and your pleasure and decision-making brain centers to get you to buy what they're selling. That's why it's important to understand how and why we humans react to the impulsive desire to buy.

Advertising is a little like the man behind the curtain in *The Wizard of OZ*. While he remained hidden, he was able to manipulate Dorothy and her companions with smoke and flame and mirrors, but once Toto pulled the curtain back and the Wizard and his tricks were revealed, he was no longer a nemesis—he became a friend.

Advertising, like the Wizard, is neither good nor bad. It *is*, for better or worse, a driving force in the world economy and without it, mass production, affordable goods and our modern lifestyle would not exist. Advertising can help you make wise buying decisions by informing you of a product's qualities or it can hinder you by misleading you into thinking a product is something it's not. Few ads are wholly informative or wholly misleading; they're usually a bit of both, and it can be hard to tell which is which. Some parts of an ad are designed to appeal to your consciousness, some parts to your gut, some parts to both. Taken as a whole, separating the wheat from the chaff can be frustratingly difficult and even impossible. But when you understand the anatomy of an advertisement, you can dissect it and tell what is true and valuable, what is superfluous fluff and what is meant to trick you into buying something you really don't want or need. Perhaps the most powerful element of any ad is the part that appeals to your gut, to your reward system and your natural human impulse to acquire things—to buy for the sheer act of buying.

We buy things to fulfill our wants and needs, but there is another component to buying that is not so easy to put your finger on. It's very basic and powerful: It's the desire to possess something just to possess it. There's something in human nature that derives pleasure from the *pure act of acquiring*, and it can be so powerful and overwhelming that we respond to it instinctively and with little or no reasoning. We sometimes react almost automatically, giving in to the impulse to buy, short-circuiting the consciousness entirely in much the same way we might, when we trip and stumble, reach out with our hands to break a fall. Even when we make carefully considered purchases, we are still vulnerable to the spell of impulse buying. It's woven into every advertisement, marketing message, package and store shelf.

Why do we derive pleasure from the act of acquiring? Could it be an atavistic trait from the time when we were hunters and gatherers, a time when survival could depend upon possessing the right object: a rock, a stick, a morsel of food? The primitive man must have always been on the lookout for things that would aid in his survival and this trait of acquiring would have been woven into his DNA. Today, while the purpose of the drive to acquire no longer exists in its original form, we still succumb to its siren call. We buy things.

This curious fact about human nature has not gone unnoticed by advertisers whose job it is to convince the buying public to purchase whatever it is they're selling. Savvy advertisers will tout their products' benefits and features, but they will also try to tap into that strange need we all have to possess things just for the sheer pleasure of acquiring. They'll tell us, "Buying is easy, buying is fun!" There's nothing wrong with the practice, but sometimes we can be so swayed that we make unwise purchase decisions, putting resources that could be better spent into things that don't especially help our chances for success or, worse yet, hurt them. That's why it's so important to understand how advertising speaks to our impulsive nature to get us to buy, buy, buy.

You know what I'm talking about. You're doing your weekly shopping at the supermarket, you have your list and you're filling your cart as you roll it up and down the aisles. Bread, milk, eggs, butter, a couple of cans of tuna fish. At the checkout counter, you wait while the person in front of you finishes up and pays. You're idly looking around, you take a magazine off the rack and flip through it. Your gaze strays to a shelf, when suddenly something catches your attention. You pause, maybe even reach out and take that something off the shelf. You look at it from a couple of different angles, read the label, admire the brightly colored packaging. If it's something to eat, you might start to feel a bit peckish. If it's a gadget, you start to envision how you might put it to use. You glance at the price tag; it's cheap. *What the heck*, you say to yourself and almost without thinking you throw it in the cart. It's something you don't need and there's a chance you'll never actually use it. You don't know why you're buying it, you just suddenly want to. The act of acquiring it provides a strange satisfaction and it makes you feel good. The pleasure derived from the simple act of buying gives you all the motive you require. You aren't moved to purchase either by need or want; you are attracted by something much more primal, primitive and powerful.

When we make a purchasing decision, we are guided by our emotions, but there is usually a reasoning process involving the conscious brain, too. There are exceptions, though. Sometimes we make a purchase not for the value of the thing itself, but for the pure pleasure of possession. I'm talking, of course, about impulse buying, and it's a psychological reality that has spawned an entire industry dedicated solely to getting us to purchase things on the spur of the moment. There's even a scientific definition for it: Impulse buying occurs when an individual makes an unintended, unreflective and immediate purchase. The person's attention is focused on the immediate gratification of responding to the urge to buy rather than on solving a preexisting problem or on finding an item to fill a predetermined need.

Quite a mouthful to explain a very simple act. Impulse buying is really just the urge to buy something that has caught the eye. For some reason we feel an overwhelming attraction to and desire for the thing, so we reach in our pockets and plunk down the money. And it's very big business. One study reports that between twenty-seven and sixty-two percent of all department store sales are the products of impulse buying.

So it's no wonder that advertisers have spent millions, perhaps billions, of dollars figuring out new ways to tap into the impulse gene for purchases both big and small. Researchers have been studying impulse buying for several decades and they've discovered some interesting things. For instance, while some people are more likely to buy on impulse than others, no one is immune to the forces that get us to buy without reasoning. That's because at the root of it, we're all basically wired alike. We all have reward systems that respond much the same way to the same stimuli. One key discovery is that browsing creates a pleasant feeling, and the more we browse, the more likely we are to buy. And so stores are purposely designed to get us to wander about and expose ourselves to the merchandise. Every part of the retail environment is taken into consideration. Visceral design cues such as colors, lighting, sound and even scent are used to get us to relax, get comfortable, drop our guard and spend our money.

Again, our old friend dopamine plays a major role in this state of mind. As we browse, we are exposed to pleasing experiences that trigger the release of dopamine. We become enthusiastic, active and alert. We're filled with positive feelings of anticipation and engagement with the environment around us. We want to be persuaded. The more we browse, the better we feel, as our brains receive greater and greater doses of dopamine. The strongest positive feelings come with proximity to a product that has suddenly become desirable—often irresistibly so. To maintain this mildly euphoric state, we imagine possessing and using the product, and bingo! We're sold.

That we are more susceptible to impulse buying when we are in a good mood should come as no surprise. After all, when we feel good we are more likely to reward ourselves generously. Yet it seems we are also more likely to buy on impulse when we are feeling blue. While being somewhat down is not as powerful a motivator as being in a good mood is, we still tend to seek out the good feeling we get from purchasing something we might not need but are manipulated by the store's environment to suddenly want. We might submit to impulse buying simply to cheer ourselves up. One study found that seventy-five percent of people reported they felt better after making an impulse purchase, while only eight percent reported feeling worse.

One of the ways advertisers activate the impulse component of the buying experience is by getting us to relate to their products on more human terms. They give them human names and create cute cartoon characters they hope we'll like and associate with their products. They understand that we are more likely to care about something we can bond with. For instance, we might think of a sleek sports car as having a sexy personality. We might see an overstuffed easy chair as having a friendly personality. When we assign certain human qualities to things, we are simply thinking of them in familiar terms of personality and we form an emotional association.

Another trick advertisers use is to show us images of people we'd like to be or associate with. For a sports drink, svelte volleyball players frolicking on a sunlit beach. For a candy bar, laughing children. For charcoal briquettes, friends gathered around the backyard barbecue. We've seen all these tactics thousands of times, and we understand the trick being played on us; still, who among us hasn't fallen for it at least once in the last month? Before you make your next impulse buy, run the item through your mental design checklist. When you take the time to evaluate it on visceral, behavioral and reflective levels, chances are you'll put that item right back on the shelf. Don't browse. Know what item or items you are looking for before you go shopping and stick to your list. Don't be distracted by flashy promotions touting limited quantities or temporary price reductions. Go straight for the item or items you need and remember to evaluate them on their qualities and how well they fit your needs. Then give them the dopamine test and see how they make you feel. It's the only way you can cut through the clutter and make a wise buying decision.

Emotional Selling

Those of us in the communication and marketing business have always known that emotions sell. And now there's a wealth of science to support what was until now an opinion based on intuition and experience. As shown in the first chapter, researchers have made a lot of progress in unraveling the mystery of love at first sight, both Big Love and Little Love. Using advanced brain-imaging techniques, they've been able to identify the parts of the brain responsible for creating that pleasurable sensation we get when we're attracted to another person. Now, using the same approaches, researchers are beginning to delve into the physiology of the impulse to buy, too. Until the results of recent research became clear, advertisers had to rely on focus groups, gross sales figures and other relatively crude metrics to judge the effectiveness of their efforts. Even ads that produce trackable direct sales numbers don't necessarily tell us why. The problem with these traditional tactics is that, at best, they provide only a rough estimate of what worked in the past and little or no guidance on what advertisers can do in the future to improve performance. But now researchers are bringing advertising and marketing into the twenty-first century by using sophisticated brain-imaging machines to map the aesthetic experience and the buying impulse. They are zeroing in on how to be more effective at getting us to buy and it's important that we as consumers are aware of what they're up to. It's interesting and not a little ironic to note that these research projects are producing cold, hard, incontrovertible data confirming that our emotions lead the way when it comes to making buying decisions, a departure from many long-held beliefs. In a study released not long ago, researchers used magnetoencephalography (MEG) to understand what happens in the brain when people make their buying decisions. Tim Ambler, a senior fellow at London Business School and co-author of "Salience and choice: Neural correlates of shopping decisions," concluded, "this [study] helps in the growing understanding of decision-making as a largely unconscious habitual process, as distinct from the rational, conscious, information-processing model of economists and traditional marketing textbooks. Feelings are more important than reason..."

Ambler's study sought to determine whether buying decisions could be linked directly to physiological processes occurring in the brain. People who took part in the study were asked to shop in a virtual supermarket and to choose products from eighteen brand categories. They were hooked up to the MEG unit so researchers could watch and record the different levels of brain activity produced by viewing different products. The subjects were asked which brand they would choose, and their brain images were then compared to what they said they preferred. The results were astounding. It turned out that their verbal choices and the choices predicted by the brain images matched up—proving that researchers can actually observe and predict with a high degree of certainty the results of the brain's decision-making process. It was almost as though by watching the test subjects' brains, scientists could actually tell whether they would chose Skippy peanut butter or Jif! However, while shedding light on the decision-making process, the study didn't specifically show *why* the test shoppers decided to buy one product instead of another.

A different study by Marco Iacoboni, a neurologist and director of the Transcranial Magnetic Stimulation Laboratory of the Ahmanson-Lovelace Brain Mapping Center at the David Geffen School of Medicine at UCLA, moves a little closer to answering the question of why. Iacoboni and his group used functional magnetic resonance imaging to study the brains of subjects as they responded to ads for Disney World, Sierra Mist (a soft drink) and three beer brands: Bud Light, Budweiser and Michelob. The ad for Disney World produced the most positive brain signals. It showed players with the Seattle Seahawks and Pittsburgh Steelers practicing the line, "I'm going to Disney World." Why did this ad elicit a stronger emotional response than the beer and soft drink ads? One possible explanation is particularly strong from a reward system perspective: A trip to Disney World for a week's vacation is a much bigger reward than a trip to the corner store for a six pack.

These and other studies give credence to what savvy advertisers have known all along: People make emotional decisions, then justify them with rational arguments—something we as consumers in search of products that will enhance our environments certainly need to be aware of.

To better understand the impulse buying factor, how to spot it in advertising and guard against its effect, it's important to discuss the strategies and tactics advertisers use. One way advertisers tickle our impulse-buying bone is to use some real feature or benefit of the product to "leverage" into a bigger, more attractive narrative that will make us desire their wares.

Perception and Reality

In his novel *The Count of Monte Cristo,* Alexandre Dumas creates the character of Edmond Dantes, a young, illiterate sailor falsely imprisoned as a traitor in post-Napoleonic France. Dantes spends years in an island dungeon, his only companion a mad priest who teaches young Dantes literature, science, geography, history and the social niceties of the privileged class. The priest also discloses the hidden location of a vast fortune of silver, gold and precious jewels. After almost twenty years, Dantes escapes from his prison cell, recovers the treasure and takes up residence in Paris as the wealthy, dashing and mysterious Count of Monte Cristo. Dantes is no more. The Count has taken his place.

Through the artful blending of perception and reality, Dantes creates a completely new identity for himself. He has lived the desperate life of a sailor and prisoner and those experiences are carved in stone upon his character. They are his realities. They provide a foundation of determination, cunning and wile even as his elegant trappings create a perception of breeding, wealth and *noblesse oblige.* By combining these characteristics, the Count has become a charismatic personality irresistible to Parisian nobility.

Through this blending of perception and reality, Dumas deftly invents an attractive, compelling personality. A few years later, another master of perception and reality will do the same, only this time it will be for a bar of soap.

Thomas Barratt and Pears Soap

In the late 1800s, most soaps contained caustic chemicals and heavy metals such as lead and arsenic. Those abrasive concoctions were notorious for causing inflammations, rashes and sores. One brand though, Pears Soap, was different. It was made from all-natural ingredients, was transparent and instead of irritating, it was gentle. It was a high-quality, limited-production soap, and not many people knew about it. But Thomas Barratt, the owner of the company that produced Pears Soap, came up with a revolutionary idea that would change all that. The result was one of the first image ads ever run in a newspaper and the launch of advertising and branding as an art and an industry.

Barratt bought exclusive rights to *A Child's World*, a painting of a cherubic, curly-haired, clear-skinned toddler by the artist Sir John Millais. He added the image of his soap to the painting and bought space for the ad in newspapers. The painting represented everything perceived to be good and pure and wholesome about childhood—exactly how Barratt wanted his soap to be seen. He blended the reality of his soap's gentleness with the perception of precious childhood to create a personality for his product that would resonate with people and get them to buy.

The painting, which later became known as *Bubbles* because of its association with Pears Soap, caught the attention of a broad audience. People naturally had an emotional connection to the child depicted in the painting, which represented gentleness and purity. And just as Barratt hoped, that feeling was extended to his soap. Countless other companies over the years have followed Barratt's lead in blending perception and reality to make an attractive personality that would create Three Second Windows for millions of people, get the dopamine flowing and generate demand for their products. An example that stands out is an ad that ran only twice, but continues to have a huge impact to this day.

Why 1984 Wasn't Like *1984*

The ad agency Chiat/Day had just won the Apple Computer account, and one of its first tasks was to create an ad to launch the Macintosh. The Mac was different from the IBM and IBM-compatible computers that dominated the marketplace at the time. The Mac had a mouse and employed a graphical user interface, a radical departure from other computers then being sold. Lee Clow was the creative director at Chiat/Day and he came up with the idea for the ad that would propel the Mac to the forefront of the world stage, make it a household word and change the way we think about and use computers from that day forward.

In 1984, the computer business was much different than it is today. IBM was the world's largest home computer maker, holding an iron-fisted monopoly over the industry. IBM was the behemoth; it made the products it felt like making and if you wanted a computer, you took what IBM had to offer. In the home computer culture, IBM was a little like Big Brother, the all-seeing, all-knowing and all-powerful antagonist in George Orwell's dystopian novel, *1984*.

Back in '84, IBM computers were still running on a DOS platform, which meant you controlled the content on your screen by typing in codes via the keyboard—a slow and awkward process. But the Mac was different. It had a mouse. You didn't have to memorize all those codes just to perform simple operations. You could get the job done with the flick of your wrist and a tap of your finger. Mac broke from the status quo; it was intuitive, it was fun and easy to use, the case even looked different. There were friendly little icons on the screen. It was the exact opposite of the IBM machine; it was *superior*. But Apple was playing David to IBM's Goliath. The Mac would have to create a spectacular Three Second Window to overcome IBM's momentum. It would need to project an attractive personality that people could understand, connect with and relate to. Clow would have to produce an ad that first and foremost went straight for the impulse gene. With the airing of his spot, all that was about to happen.

Clow's brainchild ran as a TV commercial that ran during the third quarter of the 1984 Super Bowl game between the Los Angeles Raiders and the Washington Redskins. Clow's idea was to capitalize on the notion, beginning to gain popular currency, that the future might not be quite as bright as we all once thought. Ronald Reagan's landslide election in 1980 and again in 1984 was in part a backlash against the perceived intrusive evils of Big Government. People were starting to realize the negative effect humans were having on the environment, and Cold War headlines were a constant reminder of the ever-present threat of nuclear holocaust. The future wasn't what it used to be—it was beginning to look more like the one described in *1984*.

Clow's ad begins drearily with a scene set in an auditorium, where a group of people with shaved heads and dressed in drab gray coveralls watch with dull-eyed lassitude as an Orwellian figure on a giant video screen delivers a lecture. The copy, written by Steve Hayden, is truly chilling. Big Brother speaks:

> Today, we celebrate the first glorious anniversary of the Information Purification Directives. We have created, for

the first time in all history, a garden of pure ideology, where each worker may bloom, secure from the pests purveying contradictory thoughts. Our Unification of Thought is more powerful a weapon than any fleet or army on earth. We are one people, with one will, one resolve, one cause. Our enemies shall talk themselves to death and we will bury them with their own confusion. We shall prevail!

The heroine of the 1984 ad is a familiar archetype: the brave, sole protagonist battling against overwhelming odds in defense of freedom, individuality and integrity. She is the Lone Ranger, Batman and Captain America all rolled into one. She represents Mac and is the principal player in a powerful Three Second Window. We are instantly attracted to her. We want to be like her. To be like her we need to go out and purchase a Mac. Lee Clow associated her with Apple to create an attractive personality for the Mac computer in the same way Barratt used the painting of a child to create an attractive personality for his soap. Clow's 1984 ad didn't promise any specific benefits. There were just too many to talk about in a thirty-second spot. No mention was made of the mouse or the graphical user interface. In fact, most of his ad was spent conjuring up a negative perception of the competition, one that he and, by proxy, his viewers could feel good about rebelling against.

Clow was satisfied to simply create a perception that the Mac was the smart, creative, rugged individual's alternative to IBM's stodgy, putty-colored boxes. He chose to eschew benefits and features and instead go straight for the impulse gene. He chose to position the Mac as "the computer for the rest of us," and let the viewer bring his or her own meaning to that message. The Mac was given a personality. It became the cool computer. It was attractive and desirable and people wanted one right away.

When I view this ad today, many years after I first saw it, I still feel what I've come to recognize as that little shot of dopamine. I feel the magic. My scalp tingles and the hair on the back of my neck stands up. I feel really good, elated even, when near the end, the heroine whacks the heck out of Big Brother. *Yes!* I think, *take that!* Now the dopamine is really flowing as the copy about the Macintosh rolls across the screen and that brave, clear voice assures me that Mac will make sure

"1984 won't be like *1984.*" That good feeling I have gets transferred to Apple Inc. I feel as though I have a personal connection with Apple and everything the company produces. I feel a sense of belonging and loyalty, motivation even, and I wonder if maybe I'm feeling a little of what those ancient hunters felt when they viewed the cave paintings or maybe what my mother felt when she saw the Iwo Jima photo in the newspaper back during World War II.

Personality and Positioning

Thomas Barratt positioned Pears Soap as the mild, all-natural alternative to the caustic brands then being sold. Lee Clow positioned the Mac as the computer for the rest of us. Both used their competitors as backdrops against which to showcase their products' strengths. They artfully blended perception and reality to create an appealing personality for their respective products that would activate our impulse to buy. Since the days of Thomas Barratt, positioning has been key to creating Three Second Windows that tap into the impulse to buy. In his book *Ogilvy on Advertising,* David Ogilvy talks about positioning while discussing an ad campaign he did for Saab: "In Norway, the Saab car had no measurable profile. We positioned it as a car for *winter.* Three years later, it was voted the *best* car for Norwegian winters." Ogilvy, another giant in the world of advertising, understood the need to create the perception that products have personalities, a quality people can connect to on a deep, emotional level—almost in the same way they connect to other people. Back in the early 1960s, the Beetle constituted Volkswagen's primary product line. Ogilvy says of his partner Bill Bernbach and Bernbach's ads, now known as the Think Small campaign, that "[he] and his merry men positioned the Volkswagen as a protest against the vulgarity of Detroit cars in those days, thereby making the Beetle a cult among those Americans who eschew conspicuous consumption." The Think Small campaign took what was assumed to be a shortcoming of the Beetle—its small size—and turned it into a positive character trait. The campaign gave the Beetle a personality people understood and could support.

Personality and Brand

Think about your favorite brands, the ones with personalities that best fit your own. They're the products you've learned to like better than others. Maybe it's a soft drink that has just the right amount of fizz and isn't too sweet. Or perhaps you've tried different kinds of running shoes and found that one model seems to make you faster. You're able to identify with your favorite products by the projection of their personalities through brand: the intersection of advertising, packaging, price and of course the product itself. Brand, or image, has a huge effect on how we perceive a product. Brand will determine to a large degree your expectations and enjoyment of the product. Ogilvy tells the story of a test performed to determine the effect of brand on perception. "Researchers at the department of psychology at the University of California gave distilled water to students. They told some of them that it was distilled water, and asked them to describe its taste. Most said it had no taste of any kind. They told the other students that the distilled water came out of the tap. Most of them said it tasted *horrible*. The mere mention of *tap* conjured up an image of chlorine."

Ogilvy elaborates on this theme. "Give people a taste of Old Crow, and *tell them it's Old Crow*. Then give them another taste of Old Crow *but tell them it's Jack Daniels*. Ask them which they prefer. They'll think the two drinks are quite different. *They're tasting image.*"

Old Crow is perceived as a cheaper, lower-quality whiskey, while Jack Daniels is thought of as a very high-quality product. People aren't being dishonest when they report different experiences from the same stimuli. They are simply being influenced by the advertising and letting their conscious, conditioned expectations override their reward systems.

Consistency plays a big role in the cementing of a brand. We need to be exposed to a brand many times—in a way, conditioned—before our brains learn to recognize it as having a certain personality. A recent study found that the most effective TV ads are those that get our attention quickly and are seen numerous times. The first time we view a great TV spot, one that grabs our emotions, we get that shot of dopamine and we feel good. If it's a really effective ad, one that entertains us, we want to see it again. In a small way, we become addicted to it. When we stop to watch a TV spot we've seen before, what we really crave is not the ad itself, or the product it's promoting, but the dopamine it produces and the feeling we get from thinking about possessing the product that activates our reward systems.

Brand isn't created overnight. Our brains have to be exposed to the same stimuli over and over again before it becomes an established part of its structure. Advertisers ensure this consistency through brand strategy and tactics. Although few ad and marketing agencies think of it this way, brand strategy is really about laying out a plan to create numerous Three Second Windows to trigger an audience's reward system and produce dopamine. Tactics are the specific actions that execute the strategy. Tactics can include individual ads as well as a campaign that uses a single theme, such as Marlboro's Marlboro Man or Eveready's Energizer Bunny.

Getting us to buy products by tapping into our impulsive natures has become a fine art. And now, with the introduction of advanced brain-scanning technology, it has become a science, too. As manufacturers and marketers hone their techniques to an ever-greater degree, picking out good, well-designed products by being sensitive to the way your reward system works and employing reasoned, critical analysis becomes harder—and more important every day.

Here's why: The goal of every company is to create a cadre of brand-loyal customers, shoppers who will reach for products from a certain company almost without thinking. They've had good experiences with those products or the customer service they received and feel an identification with the company that sometimes can override their critical senses. They tend to think of the company, its employees and products as friends of a sort, people and things they can rely on. Often brand-loyal shoppers will purchase from a company they feel attached to without comparing the offerings from other companies. They will assume because they've had one or two positive purchasing experiences that everything the company offers must be of similar high quality. The truth, however, is that every product has a life cycle. When a product is introduced, it might be at the forefront of the products in its category, but after a while, sometimes just a matter of months, other products from other companies come out that are a little farther along in research and development. They're better, cheaper to buy and easier to use. It's expensive to design, retool and manufacture even the simplest item, so no company's entire line will ever have the best product in every category. There will always be a mix of new, aging and downright obsolete products offered for sale. Sure, some of your favorite company's products will be superior, but that doesn't mean they all will be. Chances are another manufacturer has the same thing or better for less. That's why it's so important *not* to be brand-loyal.

Recently, I decided it was time to buy a new pair of running shoes, so I went to my favorite store to see what they had to offer. The first thing the salesperson asked me was, "What brand do you like?"

I've been running and buying running shoes for forty years and I know from experience that the best shoe is the one that fits the best. I told her, "I don't buy by brand, I buy by fit." I described my running habits, my gait and mileage and asked for a shoe that would meet my needs. She brought out five or six different shoes of various brands and I run-tested each one, ignoring the brand as much as possible. Now, I have always been partial to Nike, because that was the first brand of running shoe I ever bought back in the day, and I've had some Nikes since that were outstanding. But I put my bias on hold long enough to give each shoe the dopamine test based solely on feel not brand. I wound up with a pair of shoes that, after a month of hard wear, I'm still extremely happy with. What brand did I pick? Honestly, I'd have to go look at them to tell you.

Still, it can be an effort *not* to automatically buy from the same company over and over again. All the big companies I've ever had as clients employed entire departments devoted solely to making their customers brand-loyal. I've even helped them do it! A company will offer you reduced rates or prices, bonus points and other perks just to get you to remain its customer. This strategy produces great success for the companies employing it, but not necessarily for you as a consumer. Our natural impulse is to go for what's worked in the past. Sometimes this impulse is so strong that we don't even consider other companies' products. Don't fall for it. Shop around and evaluate and remember to let your reward system—not misleading advertising—inform your decisions.

All advertising speaks to our impulsive desire to possess something for the sheer pleasure of possessing it. Some ads rely more heavily on this "impulse gene" than others, but it's always a component. Pure impulse buying goes straight for the gut, circumvents the consciousness and confuses the reward system into releasing that shot of dopamine that sends the message *I want this!* But once you understand how impulse buying works, you're less likely to fall prey to its tactics. The next time you feel tempted to buy something on impulse, stop, take a few deep breaths and consider this: Impulse buying is really a series of rationalizations we come up with for needing the thing right now. We tell ourselves that if we don't get it immediately, the store will run out and we will have missed our chance. We might make the argument that the cost is so small that it won't impact our budgets. Or we will invent myriad uses for it. If it's an item of food, we'll convince ourselves that we're hungry when we're actually not. Or it might be some novel item we just have to try for fun. Maybe we're feeling particularly up or particularly down and are tempted to purchase to reinforce or change our mood. The reasons we come up with for impulse buying are as varied as are individual people.

Things you buy purely on impulse rarely contribute to a harmonious environment. They usually wind up in a closet or a box in the attic and eventually the landfill. By now, you've probably learned to recognize the feeling of dopamine and understand its role in Your Three Second Window. That great feeling is there to help you make wise choices, so by no means should you ignore it—even in an impulse-buying situation—but do put the product itself out of mind for a moment. Go over each reason you came up with for having to have the product at that very moment and give it the dopamine test. It's a sure-fire way to know if your reasons are valid or simply inventions meant to justify your immediate desire to buy. You'll probably put that product right back on the store shelf, which is a lot better place for it than in your stomach or your home or office.

Chapter 6

Why We Buy

The impulse to buy, to possess things, is part of being human and all advertising appeals to that nature to one degree or another. But there's more that goes into getting you to buy through advertising than that. Effective advertising works on both levels—conscious and subconscious. The people whose jobs are to sell you the things that surround you in your home and workplace have a whole bag of tricks to get you to buy. There's always a strong subconscious, impulsive component to the buying process but there are conscious components, too. Savvy advertisers recognize all the facets and they cover all their bases. They've developed tactics and strategies to lead you along the path to purchase, one Three Second Window at a time. While all buying decisions are emotional at their root, advertisers weave in message components that appeal to your conscious brain, too. Understanding the different components of a sales message gives you a leg up on the advertisers; alerted to their tactics, you are better able to see through the hype, use your reward system to help evaluate your purchase decisions and choose those things that will help you create an environment that nurtures creativity and invites success.

Along with an appeal that goes straight for your natural impulse to acquire a thing, advertisers also try to influence your conscious thought process by touting a product's benefits and features. The controversy over whether benefits or features best create desire is not a new one. It's something we in the advertising business argue about all the time. One school believes fervently that communicating a product's features is the best way to make a sale. This group is mostly on the client side. They are understandably in love with their products, know every screw, wire and microchip, and want everyone else to marvel at their product's neat high-res screen, dual-sensing diodes and multichannel capacitors.

The other school of thought resides in the creative corridors of the ad and marketing agencies. The creative crowd believes just as strongly that focusing on benefits is a more effective way to get you to buy. The reasoning is that you are much more interested in *what* a product can do for them than in *how* it does it.

A few years ago, I was creating ads for a cell phone company. We generally offered a great deal on handsets when people agreed to sign a yearlong contract. Sometimes we even gave the handsets away for free. By then, the cell phone industry had developed into a pretty level playing field. A few rare exceptions aside, phones were about the same and the service was largely equal across all companies. Still, some providers sold more, perhaps because their ads worked better.

My client was a wonderful, thoughtful and savvy person, but she and I had come to loggerheads a few times about how best to market her product. I thought it would be interesting to prove once and for all just what gets people to buy, so I proposed running a test. I created two ads that looked identical. The images were the same, the typeface and type size didn't change. The only difference was a slight adjustment of the headline. In one, my headline read "Unlimited Minutes, Unlimited Internet Access, Unlimited Opportunities"— in other words, a laundry list of features. The other headline read "Get more done," a clear, simple benefit if ever there was one. Now, all the neat things listed in the first example constituted a pretty hot feature set for the day. It's also an easy proposition to understand, and it worked well—we signed up a lot of new customers with that ad.

But the second ad, "Get more done," hit the ball out of the park. It made my client a lot more sales. Why? The answer, I believe, is that we respond differently to different kinds of input. Both ads were well written, well designed and created desire, but the one that used a benefit—the idea of getting more done—produced a stronger emotional response than the ad that led with the features. It was simply more effective at getting the dopamine flowing. Benefit-driven ads work better, I believe, because they appeal to both the subconscious reward system and to rational thought. You get two for one!

Over the years, I've performed similar tests and, without fail, the benefit-oriented ad has produced better results than the ad touting the product's features. Why do benefits work better than features? It seems to me the main reason is that benefits are more direct and require less interpretation by the subconscious and conscious brains. When you read the headline "Get more done," you instantly understand the meaning and the benefit, and the dopamine gets flowing right away. Getting more done can mean a lot of things to different people, but it will always be interpreted as something good: *I'll have more free time. I'll be more productive. I won't have to worry so much. I'll make more money.* There's no downside to getting more done. With a benefit-oriented ad, the subconscious and conscious brains have less work to do, and the response is quicker and less ambiguous.

Feature-oriented pitches, on the other hand, are more complicated. They are less clear and more muddled. You have to think about them. There's less involvement with the reward system, so the emotional draw is not as strong—it might even be completely absent. There are a lot of plusses but a lot of minuses as well. "Unlimited Minutes, Unlimited Internet Access, Unlimited Opportunities" requires a lot of thought and interpretation before you decide whether it's going to provide you with a benefit. The offer is a good one, but it leads to a lot of questions: *Do I really need that many minutes? What are they costing me? Does it include long distance? Do I really need wireless Internet? What are the other guys offering? What's the catch?* It's not that features have no place in creating desire in Your Three Second Window, they do; but they work better when used to support the benefits rather than supplant them. For instance, in the ad cited above, I used the phone plan's features to validate my benefit claim. Explaining how the phone plan would help the consumer get more done was necessary to make the benefit claim believable.

When you venture out into the marketplace to find a product that will help you create a harmonious environment, you are probably thinking mostly about how that product will fit in with and enhance your life. You are probably more interested in how the thing looks and works than in how it does its job, so it's only natural that you will respond more positively to its set of benefits than you will to its set of features. And that's as it should be. But remember, sometimes an ad will tout a set of benefits that sounds good and will cause you to want to buy. A word of caution: Make sure the ad substantiates those benefits with real features and that they are understandable and make sense.

Context in a Crowded World

I read somewhere that the average American is exposed to five thousand marketing and advertising messages every day. That seemed like a lot to me until I started to add them up. Let's see—there are the ads you see and hear on TV and radio in the morning and evening. Calculate in the number of billboards, bus banners, truck and car signs and all the other outdoor advertising you see on your way to work. Then, as you settle into your office or cubicle, chances are pretty good that there are a lot of ads and company promotional messages on the items in your work space: software boxes, giveaways, maybe even a company logo on the pen you use. When you log onto your computer, a couple dozen junk e-mails are waiting for you. You visit a Web site for the news or to do some research and you're assailed with more banner and pop-up ads. Finally, back at home (after passing all that outdoor advertising for a second time), you go to the refrigerator for a well-deserved libation, and guess what? More ads and marketing messages. Even the milk carton you brought home from the store is trying to sell you something else. Thankfully, you are able to fly right past most of these messages; they simply form a mildly irritating background noise.

We've evolved to ignore everything except those things that our reward systems interpret as either providing an advantage for, or posing a threat to, our survival. For instance, you probably wouldn't pay much attention to the ad on the back of the truck that's ahead of your car, but that same image would become very important to you if the truck swerved and stopped suddenly. Thanks to evolution, you're able to very quickly look at all the people, events and things that make up your environment, compare them with one another and determine which ones are worthy of your attention.

Think back to our group of intrepid Paleolithic hunters. As they stalk the herd of bison, they need to evaluate each animal quickly and choose the ones that represent the best opportunities for harvest. The hunters no doubt would take many factors into account: the health of each animal, its size and difficulty of the kill in relationship to the others in the herd. They would choose those animals that compare most favorably with the other animals around them. An animal judged inferior in a herd of very large and healthy bison might be considered a prime target in a herd of lesser animals. How you perceive desirability depends to a great extent upon context. Advertisers know this and have a whole bag of tricks to get your attention for their products while blocking out their competitors' messages.

Your subconscious brain is very adept at grouping together the things that form your environment. Cars belong to the set of vehicles. Bus banners and billboards belong to the advertisement group. People belong to the human race. You automatically categorize the people and things around you in order to give some higher priority, some lower. When you group people and things together, you tend to assign not only importance, but value as well. Some people and things are more important to your survival than others and your brain treats them accordingly. Based on their survival value, you tend to like some groups better than others. For instance, your reward system is more likely to give you a shot of dopamine when you see someone who belongs to the group of attractive strangers rather than to the group of *unattractive* strangers. The same subconscious process works across the board—sorting, comparing, categorizing and assigning importance and value to everything you come in contact with. Psychologists call this phenomenon *context dependence*, and it is a powerful force in your everyday life, especially in the perception of quality in the things you purchase and surround yourself with.

The Halo Effect

When I was an assistant professor in the design department of the School of Visual Arts at Penn State University, one of my duties was to participate in portfolio reviews to decide which students would be admitted into the graphic design program. It was my job, along with other professors, to determine which portfolios were of high quality and which were of lower quality. As at most schools, admittance to the design program at Penn State was highly competitive. Only about one-third of the students who wanted in were actually accepted. After participating in a few portfolio reviews, I began to notice an interesting phenomenon: When the first project in a student's portfolio was good or excellent, the projects that followed seemed to be better, too. It was as though that first impression affected my evaluation of everything that student produced. I believe that if I had seen that same excellent example farther along in the portfolio, it would not have had the same effect on the whole body of work.

This phenomenon is a common one—you've probably experienced it yourself—and it even has a name: Its called the halo effect, and psychologists say it has a very strong influence on how we make decisions about what we like and what we don't. Understanding this principle helps you see through advertising tactics that employ the halo effect and make better buying decisions, too. The halo effect got its name from a researcher in the nineteen twenties, Edward Thorndike. Thorndike observed that people tended to put a lot of emphasis on looks and personality when judging another person's capabilities. Attractive people were routinely perceived as more able, smarter and of higher character than those who were perceived as less attractive. That's why you rarely see an unattractive person speaking in behalf of a product on TV.

Real estate agents are familiar with the halo effect and many use it in their businesses. It's not uncommon for an agent to show the house he or she wants to sell first, then show the prospective buyer lesser houses—making the first one look even better in comparison.

The Contrast Effect

"According to Jim" is a TV sitcom starring Jim Belushi, who falls into the heavier end of the height/weight ratio. He looks quite portly when filmed in a scene with his slim, attractive sitcom wife, yet he seems much thinner when seen next to the shorter, more rotund actor who plays his best buddy. Belushi hasn't gained or lost weight between station breaks, but our perception of him—along with his ability to stimulate our reward systems—simply changes as his context changes.

We consciously or subconsciously compare and contrast people and things, and we wind up making judgments about them based not wholly on the individual, but also on the individual's relationship to the other people and things around him or her. Psychologists call this the contrast effect, and Scott Plous writes about it in his book *The Psychology of Judgment and Decision Making*. "One of the most interesting studies of the contrast effect was published by Stanley Coren and Joel Miller (1974). Coren and Miller noted that a 5-foot 10-inch sports announcer looks very short when interviewing a team of basketball players, but looks very tall when interviewing racehorse jockeys. At the same time, the apparent size of the announcer does not shrink when the announcer is standing beside a large racehorse—or for that matter, a stadium.

"From this observation, Coren and Miller speculated that the contrast effect only occurs when the contrasted stimuli are similar to one another."

So, according to the contrast effect theory, although Jim Belushi would seem to gain and lose weight depending on the size of the people around him, he probably wouldn't look any slimmer next to a dump truck or any heavier next to a Porsche. Advertisers will often use the contrast effect to position their products against other products from other companies. They'll compare certain benefits and features in which their product is strong against the rival product's perceived weaknesses. These kinds of contrasts can—through clever wording and visuals—be misleading, so it's important to take that into account when viewing ads of this sort. Make sure apples are being contrasted to apples and not to oranges.

The Primacy Effect

It's said you never forget your first time. Your first drink, your first airplane ride, the first time you kissed. First times leave indelible imprints upon our psyches that stay with us throughout our lives. The power of firsts also works in smaller, everyday ways. The first word in a sentence sets up our expectations for the words that will follow. The first sentence does the same for the following paragraph and so on. Being first means having a greater power to persuade and to stand out from the crowd. In the parlance of psychology, this is called the primacy effect, and Plous cites a study by researcher Solomon Asch that demonstrates its power to influence decision making: "In this experiment, Asch asked subjects for their impressions of [other subjects]. Half the subjects were asked about someone who was *envious, stubborn, critical, impulsive, industrious,* and *intelligent.* The other half were asked about someone with the very same characteristics, except that the characteristics were presented in the opposite order: *intelligent, industrious, impulsive, critical, stubborn,* and *envious.*

"What Asch found was that the characteristics appearing early in each series influenced impressions more strongly than the characteristics appearing later."

Another example of the primacy effect is prioritizing. Think about how you make a shopping list. What do you write down first? It's probably the item that first comes to mind, which is probably the item most important to you. As you add items to the list, you might notice that things are coming to mind in descending order of importance. After a while you have to scratch your head and think harder of what items you want, because those are the things you can more easily do without.

Advertisers use the primacy effect to make their messages "sticky." They will almost always lead with the most attractive thing about their product, then restate it several times in slightly different ways. Even in a short, fifteen-second broadcast ad or half-page print ad, you'll see this tactic used. The theory is that repeating a single benefit, feature or theme will cause it to stick in your mind—in a way to condition your reward system to respond to the message component positively with the release of dopamine. Be aware of this tactic and isolate it the next time you see it. This way you can give it the dopamine test upon initial exposure—before it's had a chance to sink in and get sticky—and you'll make a better buying decision.

As we've seen, context dependence wields a powerful influence on how we feel about people and things. We tend to judge them by the company they keep. People and things that belong to certain groups we perceive as positive gain status from their group, while those people and things we see as attractive lend some of their cachet to the group as a whole. The flip side is just as true. We tend to judge more negatively any person or thing that belongs to a group we perceive as generally negative. Understanding the effects of context dependence arms you with the ability to make good judgments about the things you choose to shape your environment.

An Encounter at a Wedding

A few years ago, I was at a friend's wedding. During the reception, I found myself seated at the same table as the minister who performed the ceremony. He was an older gentleman with silver hair. He seemed kind and gentle and we struck up a conversation. "So," he said, "how do you know the bride?"

"I work with her," I replied.

"Really," he said, "what kind of work do you do?"

"Advertising."

He brightened. "Advertising? Have I seen any of your work?"

I smiled. "If you have a mailbox, you might have."

I could see the wheels turning in his head. He thought a moment, then frowned. "You," he said, "you're the guy who sends me all that junk mail!" His demeanor took a dark turn.

"No, no," I said, defensively, "really, at my agency we do only very targeted, high-end stuff..."

He didn't seem to hear. "I got a letter in the mail the other day," he growled. "Looked like something from the IRS, I thought I was being audited."

"Well, we don't..."

He interrupted me. "I almost had a heart attack. When I opened it up, it was from a DVD club. Ten movies for a dime!" He gave me an ugly look. "I don't even have a DVD player!"

I can't say I blame him for venting. The kindly minister was just doing what came naturally and lumping me in with what he considered a very negative group: direct marketers. What he didn't know is that I don't do junk mail because I don't like it either, especially the really evil kind that tries to trick you or scare the daylights out of you.

I let my minister friend in on a little secret, a quick way to tell trick junk mail from the real thing. "Look at where the stamp goes in the upper right corner," I said. "If it's genuine, it will have the words 'First Class' in the indicia, or it might have a stamp. If it says 'Standard Mail,' it's bulk and you can be sure it's a phony—pure junk mail."

We all have a generally negative view of junk mail. But it's only a subgroup of a group that we see as good, which is mail in general. People *do* like to get some kinds of mail. Letters from friends and loved ones are always welcome, and who doesn't get a little thrill when that income tax refund shows up? Sadly, we've all been misled at one time or another by junk mail that suggests there's a check inside or uses some other ruse, such as "immediate action required" or "cancellation pending." Junk letters that masquerade as something else just to get us to open them are particularly bad. They're dishonest and insulting. A lot of junk mail, though, is not so nefarious—it's just ugly. You know the stuff I'm talking about, with lots of big type shouting "Dollars Off!" or "Limited-Time Offer." These aren't exactly evil, just a little irritating. The good part is that we recognize them immediately and we know what to do with them. Our mailboxes are interesting microcosms of our bigger environments. Just as in our "real worlds," there exists a rich context of all kinds of personalities, appearances, opportunities and potential threats. Some of the characters stand out in good ways, some in bad and some are just background noise.

And of course there are those rare occasions when we are actually happy to receive an ad or piece of marketing mail; it stands out from the junk and is instantly attractive and desirable because it's interesting or visually stimulating or it might make us laugh or engage us in a subject of particular interest. Its unexpectedness within its context makes it all the more enjoyable. That's the kind of mail I love to create, and it took me a good hour of animated conversation to convince the minister that I wasn't such a bad guy after all. In fact, by the end of the evening, I had become one of a very select and highly considered group: his friends.

We all tend to put more trust in people we know than in strangers. Friends, after all, have our best interests at heart. They've displayed their affection and goodwill and so we give more weight to their opinions. We also want to please them—which is something that hasn't gone unnoticed by salespeople all over the world.

The Expensive Cheap Camera

A few summers ago, I was walking down the street in Times Square in Manhattan. It was the end of a long, hot day, and I was stopped in front of one of the many camera stores, idly perusing the window display, when a salesman sauntered out. "Hey," he said, "it's air-conditioned inside, why don't you come on in and cool down?"

I smiled. "That's okay, I'm just looking."

"Nah," said the salesman, "you look hot. I'm just heading home; you can stand right inside the door here while I close up."

I shrugged and thought *Well, why not, after all, it is pretty hot.* So I stepped inside, and the breeze from the dozen or so fans situated around the store felt good.

The salesman went back behind the counter and busied himself locking cabinets, putting away boxes. He wasn't paying much attention to me. "You from out of town?" he said after a few moments.

"Uh-huh," I replied, still wary and not wanting to get into a conversation with him.

"West Coast?"

"Seattle," I nodded.

"Some pretty country out there, I hear, some big mountains. My sister lives in Oregon."

I said nothing to that, and I was getting ready to leave when the salesman came out from behind the counter. "Hey, you gotta see this." He had a small, chrome camera in his hand, held flat-palmed as though it were something precious. "It's the tiniest damn movie camera I ever saw." He held it up, put it to his eye and began to film me. He handed it to me. "Press this little button here." A tiny screen popped out and about four seconds of video of me standing in the doorway with a dumb look on my face played. I had to admit it was an amazing little machine…

Ten minutes later, I walked out with nine hundred dollars worth of camera. I stood there in front of the store wondering what had happened. Buying an expensive miniature video camera was the last thing I had intended to do, yet there it was. I was genuinely puzzled at how I had wound up with the thing. Later, when I got back to Seattle, I found the same camera at a local shop for about two hundred dollars.

How had I been so thoroughly taken to the cleaners? I had always considered myself a shrewd shopper, yet this salesman had literally plucked me off the street and within a matter of fifteen minutes sold me a cheap camera for more than four times its worth. The worst part was that within a year, the thing quit working. It now sits in my desk drawer as a reminder to never again get played. Still, I'm sure there will come a time when some clever salesperson will manage to sell me some cheap piece of merchandise for a lot more than it's worth.

If we go back and analyze what happened, my mistakes are glaring. I'm sure you spotted them right away. The biggest mistake I made, I think, was to pay too much attention to the salesperson and not enough to the camera itself. He had given me something—a cool, comfortable place to stand—and I felt obliged to give him something in return—conversation. Once he engaged me in conversation about my home and my family, he had established a kind of friendship with me and so I was open to being persuaded. He had tapped into my reward system, my subconscious, and my conscious brain by posing as a friend. He showed me one little trick the camera could do and built a whole story around that one feature. "When you get this home, all your friends are going to want one just like it," he told me. I have to admit, the camera was a well-designed piece of equipment on the outside. The manufacturer had taken extra care to make it attractive. In terms of reflective design, it scored a ten. It had a nice, expensive-looking, polished metal finish, with a neat little hinged screen that flipped out and rotated three hundred and sixty degrees. I think the price had something to do with it, too. The fact that it was so small yet cost nearly a thousand dollars made me think that it must be of high quality. There was probably some vanity involved as well; I remember thinking at the time that my friends wouldn't be able to afford something this nice.

My second mistake came with my evaluation of the camera itself. I was taken in by its visceral and reflective design; it looked great and its cost gave it a certain cachet. I didn't pay much attention to its behavioral design, though, and that's where I fouled up the most. Had I taken the time to live with the camera for a while, I would have spotted its behavioral design flaws (as I did a few hours after purchase). It really didn't work very well. The resolution was poor, and it would dock only with a Windows-based machine. I work and play on a Mac, so I was unable to import any movies into my desktop computer. I had to use a low-powered laptop that ran Windows, which meant I rarely did more with the movies I took than view them on the camera's little screen. Another behavioral design flaw was the docking station. In order to charge the little bugger or connect it with a computer or any other viewing device, I had to lug around an unwieldy docking station that was bigger than the camera itself, which pretty much negated the compact benefit that it seemed to possess on first blush. I'm sure that the manufacturer and the salesman knew of these design flaws, but were able to generate a nice profit by disguising the shortcomings through surface treatments. What hooked me initially, I think, was the smallness of the camera. Imagine a full-featured video camera not much larger than a cigarette lighter. Right away, I thought it must be based on some new miniature micro or nano technology that was far and away advanced over anything I'd ever seen. In fact, the technology of this gadget was old, and its compactness was possible only because many of the features usually found in a video camera were either absent or transferred to the docking station. There are many compact cameras available today not much bigger than the one I bought a few summers ago, and they are in fact marvels of modern technology, but they weren't around in those days. The compact job I bought was designed to impersonate the real thing before there was a real thing. We all expect that cameras, cell phones, computers and other electronics will continue to get smaller and lighter and provide more functionality. And we "early adopters" just can't wait to be the first kid on the block. There's a whole section of the electronics industry that preys on early adopters to sell us junk posing as something that isn't quite technically possible yet.

From the salesman's perspective, it was a perfectly crafted Three Second Window, hitting on all eight cylinders. But for me, it was a perfectly crafted fleecing.

It's easy to get fooled when you want to get fooled, but if you take the time to evaluate every product you buy on all three design levels, visceral, behavioral and reflective, you'll make wiser purchase decisions every time.

Remember, visceral design has to do with the appearance of a product. Visceral design factors are meant to get our initial attention and move us toward desire to own. Behavioral design has to do with how the product actually performs. Does it do what it's supposed to? Is it easy and comfortable to use? Is it dependable and easy to maintain? Reflective design has to do with a product's image. Think back to the Rolex watch, which is rich in reflective design factors.

Most of us consumers tend to think of a product and the selling of that product as two distinctly different things, when in reality they are closely intertwined. How we feel about products plays an important role in our perception of them, and sales strategies are often based on this fact. Salespeople know how to create Three Second Windows that get us more emotionally involved because it helps them make the sale. And this isn't always bad. After all, it's not the car or the house or the clothes we crave, it's the feeling that comes with possessing those things that we're after. What could be wrong with feeling good about a purchase? A thoroughly well-designed product that fulfills all three levels of design will enhance our feeling of well-being long after the newness has worn off and will help us be more successful in everything we do. It's said that a good product at the right price will sell itself and to some degree, that's true. Sadly, many manufactured goods fall short in one way or another and require some assistance from a salesperson. Part of the salesperson's job is to cover up the flaws or distract us from noticing them, but they always show up in time. More often than not, the flaws are small and create little more than everyday frustration. But sometimes, they are so big and consequential that they make the whole world sit up and take notice.

Selling the Challenger

With an estimated two and a half million parts, NASA's space shuttle is arguably the most complicated machine ever built. But its complexity goes far beyond the realm of rivets, wires and O-rings to encompass economics, politics and even war. The National Aeronautics and Space Act of 1958 envisions a program dedicated to the peaceful exploration of space. Section 102(a) states that "the Congress hereby declares that it is the policy of the United States that activities in space should be devoted to peaceful purposes for the benefit of mankind." The act doesn't specifically put space off limits to military activities, but it places those activities under the Department of Defense. NASA's original intent was purely civilian. Still, under the Nixon administration, when the space shuttle program was just beginning, that thinking shifted. In his book *Challenger Revealed, An Insider's Account of How the Reagan Administration Caused the Greatest Tragedy of the Space Age*, Richard C. Cook writes, "Nixon's public formulation of his space policy did not mention military priorities. Behind the scenes, however, a different scenario was unfolding. NASA and the Nixon administration were already viewing the not-yet-approved shuttle as a large, versatile spacecraft for both civilian and military uses." This change of direction meant that the original design of the shuttle had to change drastically. It had to be bigger to handle large military payloads. It was also envisaged that eventually the shuttle would launch from Vandenberg Air Force Base in California, which meant—owing to Vandenberg's greater distance from the equator and colder temperatures than at the Kennedy Space Center in Florida—the shuttle would need to be lighter and have more boost at takeoff to escape the Earth's gravity while carrying those heavier payloads. Adding military missions meant that the shuttle would have to fly more often, too, which put pressure on an already strained turnaround schedule. A civilian-only space shuttle would have pushed technological boundaries. Including a military function would push them past their breaking points.

Though a lot of parts go into the construction of the space shuttle, the basic components come down to three principal systems: the shuttle itself and its three main rocket engines, the large cryogenic fuel tank upon which the shuttle appears to sit and a pair of solid-fuel rocket boosters that flank either side of the shuttle. During takeoff, the shuttle's main engines draw fuel from the fuel tank to provide thrust, aided by the rocket boosters, which burn out and are jettisoned, then reused once they are retrieved from the ocean. Simple in concept, but incredibly complex in execution, the shuttle program posed technological, administrative and organizational challenges on a scale never before confronted.

The whole idea behind the space shuttle was that it would be a "space transportation system," an inexpensive way to travel to and from orbit on a regular schedule, much like an airline. The shuttle would carry people, equipment and military hardware into space. Since the shuttle is capable of achieving only a low Earth orbit, it would also need to carry a second rocket, called the Centaur, in its cargo bay to boost military equipment to higher polar orbits. The small fleet of space shuttles would also be called upon to ferry parts of the proposed space station for astronauts to assemble in orbit. Once the space station was complete, it would be up to the shuttle fleet to support it with people, supplies and equipment. The shuttle fleet would be very busy indeed.

So that NASA and the Department of Defense could begin their ambitious schedule as soon as possible, it became important to move the shuttle from experimental to operational status in a short time. In addition, there was pressure from Congress to contain costs and budget overruns. Much of the technology was new and had to be tested in actual flights. There were problems with the main engine, tank valves and of course the notorious O-rings, to name just a few. As Cook writes, engineers "held their breath" every time a shuttle launched. Even though NASA called the shuttle operational, at the time of the *Challenger* explosion the craft was still really a flying test bed with many unresolved problems.

As we all know today, O-ring failure due to low temperatures in the right solid-fuel rocket booster was responsible for the *Challenger* disaster, but according to Cook, it was just a matter of time before some critical system failed and brought a shuttle down. It seems in retrospect that there was just too much being asked of the shuttle. The Reagan administration envisioned the shuttle as the main tool for testing and deploying the Strategic Defense Initiative, popularly known as Star Wars. Implementation of Star Wars called for twenty-four shuttle flights a year. Actual shuttle flights never reached anywhere near that number.

While it remains a feat of technological wizardry, the shuttle's expected capabilities overreached its design parameters. Had its purpose been narrower, if it had been designed and built solely for civilian purposes instead of for more demanding military use, perhaps the scope of problems would have been smaller and more easily handled. Of course, this is speculation, but the *Challenger* disaster serves to make a dramatic point about how things should and shouldn't be designed.

The Canoe Hat

What lesson from the *Challenger* disaster can we apply to our everyday lives? After all, few of us will ever get the chance to travel into space. Many problems contributed to the shuttle disaster; the failed O-ring was simply the straw that broke the camel's back. The simple truth is that the purpose of the shuttle was defined so broadly that technology just couldn't provide a wide enough range of capabilities and still create a craft that was safe and reliable. Many everyday products have the same basic fault. They just try to do too darn much!

There used to be a humor magazine called *The National Lampoon*. Every so often, it would produce a spoof on small-town Sunday newspapers called the *Dacron Republican Democrat*. The thing was hilarious, and I remember finding the ad section particularly funny. One that has stuck with me all these years was an ad for something called a Canoe Hat. The illustration showed a man walking along wearing a big hat resembling a small canoe. I don't remember the exact copy but the gist was that you could wear this contraption all day, then take it off, turn it over and use it as a boat! It's conceivable that such a thing could exist, but it wouldn't make a very good hat, or a very good canoe. Of course, the Canoe Hat takes the idea of multifunction to a ridiculous extreme, but it makes the point very well: The more specialized a thing's design, the more effectively it will perform. The less specialized a thing's design, the less effectively it will perform.

There's something appealing about products that do a lot of different things, and they're generally easier to sell. It's like getting something for free, and we're instantly attracted to those products that offer multiple functions. Wouldn't it be great, the reasoning goes, if I could buy a gadget that does two or three things instead of just one? Just think of how much money I'll save. This pitch appeals to our reward systems and our conscious brains. Talk about desirable! The problem lies in the number of compromises that have to be made to add functions. Now, I'm not saying the Swiss Army knife isn't a handy little thing to have on a camping trip. It does a lot and, with a little practice, most of the functions can be performed reasonably well, though not nearly as nicely or easily as with a single, dedicated tool. If you've ever tried to open a bottle of wine with the corkscrew on a Swiss Army knife, you know what I mean. On the other hand, some functions are so closely related that very little compromise is needed to combine them into one product. A screwdriver with interchangeable heads is a good example. The same twisting motion is at the heart of the function and that doesn't change whether you're working on a flat-blade or Phillips-head screw. But some functions are so at odds with each other that to design a single product that will perform them all requires so many design compromises as to make the thing almost—and in some cases totally—useless. You know the kind of gadgets I'm talking about. Those marvels in the infomercials on late-night TV provide some examples. The Veg-O-Matic comes to mind, along with the Pocket Fisherman and of course "Saturday Night Live's" classic spoof, the Bass-O-Matic (it uses the whole bass!).

So does this mean you should avoid multifunctional products like the plague? No, of course not. A lot of products perform more than one function and do it well, but generally those functions are so closely related that combining them doesn't represent a huge design barrier. But beware of those gadgets that cross the line and try to combine functions that are so at odds as to make the thing practically useless. Earlier in this chapter, we explored the idea of features and benefits. Generally, there is a benefit associated with a feature, but in some instances there are so many features that the benefits can actually disappear.

The pros and cons of multifunctionality seem to be universal. They apply not only to manufactured goods, but to communication as well. At my agency, we sometimes have clients who want us to load up their ad or brochure with everything but the kitchen sink. They want to tell the history of the company, name everything about every product, include each and every employee's life story and, oh yeah, it needs to make a sale, too. We call these kinds of ads Canoe Hats, because in trying to accomplish too much, they accomplish nothing.

Learning to master Your Three Second Window by using your reward system in conjunction with your conscious mind leads to sounder buying decisions and more harmonious home and work environments that invite, rather than inhibit, success. The trick is learning how to isolate the individual components of a product or an ad and give them the dopamine test. Focus on one aspect with your consciousness while disregarding all the rest and see what your reward system is telling you. In the first six chapters of this book, you've had the opportunity to perform exercises that teach you how to spot those things and people who will provide you with opportunities for success and apply that knowledge to everyday situations. Congratulations! You are well on your way to turning your everyday moments into new opportunities for success.

Part Three: The Business of Success

Chapter 7

Strategy for Success

Chances are, your life is more diverse than ever. You are probably busier at work, at home and in your social life. Sometimes this hectic pace leads to fragmentation. You might be very successful in one sphere, but less so in others. Fragmentation leads to dissatisfaction, and you might try to overcome your woes by working harder at those spheres of your life in which you feel deficient. This strategy rarely works; instead, it leads to frustration, further fragmentation and *less* success. What you need is a common thread; a way to bridge the gaps between your different "lives" and create a harmonious wave of success that permeates your whole existence. The answer lies in the myriad choices you make each day. The answer lies in each Three Second Window.

In the first two sections of this book, we explored how your reward system works in Your Three Second Window to guide you in beneficial directions in your relationships with other people and in your relationships with your physical environments. In the next three chapters, we'll explore how to be more successful in your career by learning how to use Your Three Second Window to create more effective communication with your colleagues, your clients and customers. And I'll share with you my thirty years of communication experience as a teacher and practitioner of Your Three Second Window.

You Know You Need It

Whether you're CEO of a corporation or a single entrepreneur, whether your job involves talking with people and creating documents or working behind the scenes in a technical or support capacity, the ability to present your point of view in a compelling way is vital to having a full, rewarding and successful career.

A rare few of us are blessed with the ability to communicate very effectively without having to plan or even think about it much. Some people are excellent extemporaneous speakers who can jump up in front of a crowd and deliver a compelling presentation on whatever topic comes to mind. Some writers are so adept they can win over their readers by the sheer force of their prose. I know designers who can whip out an ad or create a room complete with furniture, textures and colors through pure intuition. But for most people, creating good, strong communication efficiently and in a decent amount of time is something of a mystery. The happy truth is that the secret to good communication in any form is really no secret at all. It all has to do with planning.

My father was a plumber by profession, a carpenter by inclination and a planner by necessity. He grew up on a farm in Missouri and during his childhood, the basics of life were scarce and highly valued. In those Depression-era days, he had to make do with what he had. Waste in any form was unacceptable, and he learned the hard way to be efficient in everything he did. Whether it was plowing a field, harvesting a crop or building a barn, everything had to be carefully planned in advance. I remember him telling me when I was a boy, "If you can't draw it, you can't build it." Though I "build" communication instead of barns, that lesson has served me well through the years. In my business we call it having a strategy for success.

Strategy is at the heart of any good communication piece and so should be the starting point. It provides you with structure and direction. It enables you to organize your thoughts, plan your actions and see the dead ends before you spend frustrating hours wandering down blind alleys. Having a strategy gives you focus, so you can zero in on the task at hand and create communication that is compelling and uses Your Three Second Window in a way that is most beneficial. Whether you're preparing a speech, creating a PowerPoint* presentation, or writing a sales document or something a bit snazzier, such as an invitation, announcement or ad, it's important that you have a strategy in place before you begin creating the piece. The mistake so many people make is to approach the process from the wrong end. They start by laying out pages with copy, photos, charts and graphs, but with only a general idea of what they actually want to accomplish. In fine art, it's okay to work this way, it's an accepted method of exploration. When creating a painting, sculpture or montage, for instance, the *process* is often the goal; whatever happens, happens. But in the business of communication, if you don't have a clear, concise, well-thought-out plan, the result will be muddled, confusing and frustrating for you and your audience. You will waste Your Three Second Window and it will be hard for you to create communications that contribute to your success.

Just as elevation and plan views serve as guides for building a barn, the strategy serves as a blueprint for building communication. A good strategy also provides a yardstick with which to measure the success of the final product. It's been said that a problem well defined is a problem half solved. We take this old saw to heart at our agency. We have a standard strategy structure that guides our hands in all our projects. Whether it's a postcard or a yearlong marketing campaign, nothing happens creatively until the strategy is in place. Our strategies have different content for different clients and different products, but this in common: Every strategy answers the following critical questions:

- What to say?
- Whom to say it to?
- How to say it?

The actual structure of our strategies follows a fairly regular form that is designed to take advantage of Your Three Second Window. It has parts that fit together to create a cohesive whole. We call the first part of the strategy the situation statement. The situation statement lays out the reason for creating the communication by describing the convergence of time and circumstances that leads to an ideal opportunity for the communication to occur. An example might be that a downturn in the real estate market (time) coincides with the development of Internet sales tools (circumstances) that make it easier for real estate agents to sell properties (opportunity). Every situation statement will be different but should include at least these basics.

Once the reason for creating the communication has been described, it's time to define the goal. The goal might be to increase sales or to swing public opinion on some important topic. It could be to increase awareness of you or your company or to explain some new concept or technology. No matter the goal, it's important to spell it out in a way that is clear and concise—and to keep it to just one major goal. While there might be one or two secondary goals, it's important that they be closely associated and support and leverage the primary goal. It's fairly easy to have that kind of sharp focus when working alone, but in a group, different people will have different viewpoints on what a particular communication should accomplish. Often these viewpoints are at odds with each other. Conflicting goals can cancel each other out, and too many goals will clutter the communication and reduce its effectiveness. Talk it out with the group and come to consensus on what needs to be achieved. Many times, you'll find that one communication won't fit everyone's needs. This is the time to learn that and to plan for a second or third communication. Resist the temptation to add too many goals or make the goal so broad as to be meaningless. Remember, the narrower the goal, the more successful the communication will be in taking advantage of Your Three Second Window.

Every communication has a personality. Sometimes it grows naturally out of the content, sometimes it's planned out in advance, but most often—in the absence of a good strategy—it happens by accident. The accidental personality is inevitably disorganized, confused and boring. That's why it's so important to think about what kind of personality you want your communication to have and to include that in the strategy. We call this exercise "tone and manner," and we use it to describe the voice in which we want to speak and the look and feel we want to project. It helps to think of your communication as having the same traits a person does. Do you want your communication's personality to be fun and lighthearted—zany even—like Jim Carrey? Or should it be enticing and sultry like Angelina Jolie? Perhaps you're going for a noble, statesmanlike personality, a Nelson Mandela. If you work for a company, the tone and manner are probably going to have to fall within certain limits dictated by brand guidelines; still, it's possible to inject a healthy dose of soul into a communication bounded by even the strictest regulations.

Another way to think about tone and manner is through positioning. How does your communication fit in the larger world of communication? Does it have more substance than a thirty-second TV ad but less than *Doctor Zhivago*? Will it be lively and animated like *Fantasia* or filled with wisdom like *The Prophet*? Decide where your communication fits in. Try to find a gap in the spectrum of other, similar communications and fill it in a way that no one else has thought of. Think what style of communication best fits your message and your audience and describe it in words that are clear, simple and understandable to everyone.

Once you've settled on tone and manner, attention should be turned toward the target audience. This is a crucial step often overlooked. When I begin a project, the first thing I ask a client is, "Whom do you want to reach?"

Many times the answer is everyone.

I understand that companies want to sell as much of their product or service as they can and so they often assume that they must cast as wide a net as possible. The problem is that by targeting everyone, they are targeting no one. It's impossible to create a Three Second Window that's going to work for everyone in the world. The savvy communicator knows that the more specific he or she can be with a message, the more effective it will be. As a marketer, I always try to speak to people as individuals, not as members of a group. A handy way to do this is to create a detailed profile of your ideal audience member. Why is this person interested in what you have to say? Will your communication solve a problem he or she has? Does he or she have a particular belief you are trying to reinforce? Maybe you're trying to dissuade an opinion he or she holds. Think about age, income, interests. What kind of pastimes does he or she enjoy? Is he or she in a specific business or profession? Where does he or she live? The list of possible traits is endless, but you need concern yourself only with those that will affect your communication. Be thorough enough to create a profile with depth and personality. When you have a specific individual in mind, it's much easier to communicate in a way that will resonate with the audience.

We use two approaches to define our target audiences, and we include both of them in our strategies. The first is a simple, bare bones description. For instance, we might say that our ideal audience is twenty-five to fifty years old, homeowners earning a hundred thousand dollars or more per year, married with children. This is what we call a demographic description. It tells us generally what our target audience is like, which helps us focus. But the really valuable insight comes from what we call the If/Then list.

The If/Then list is an exercise that lets us get inside our target audience's heads and understand their thoughts as they relate to the message we want them to absorb. We present assumptions we believe to be true, then follow up each assumption with a conclusion. "Ifs" are facts known about the target audience. "Thens" are statements about how those facts can be used to increase the effectiveness of our communication. For instance, let's say you're making a presentation to a group of real estate agents about a new Internet sales tool for their industry. Your If/Then list might start out something like this:

> *If:* Target audience does not know who I am.
>
> *Then:* I need to establish myself as an authority on Internet real estate sales.
>
> *If:* Target audience is made up of experienced real estate agents.
>
> *Then:* I don't need to bore everyone by explaining sales basics.
>
> *If:* Target audience doesn't understand how the Internet can be used to improve sales.
>
> *Then:* I should start out by explaining Internet sales step by step.

When it comes time to actually create the communication, this If/Then list will prove invaluable. You'll be able to refer to the list and create parts of the communication to address each item. A critical thing to keep in mind is to avoid "weasel words" in the If/Then list—words such as most, some, might, could, probably and maybe. For instance, a useless If statement might look like these:

> *If:* The target audience **probably** doesn't know who I am.
>
> *If:* **Most** of the target audience is composed of experienced real estate agents.

It's impossible to create Then statements that complete If statements like those above. The problem becomes how do you *probably* talk to *most* of your audience? You have to speak to *all* of your audience the same way. You must assume either everyone or no one knows who you are. Either all are experienced or none is experienced. Remember, you are communicating your message to individuals. You can't assume a person both knows and doesn't know you. An individual can't be both experienced and inexperienced at the same time. When it comes to the If/Then list, it's all or none.

Of course, there will be times when it's not possible to tightly define your target audience or to segment it into groups with which you can communicate separately. In those cases, there are still ways to speak to them as individuals. One thing they will all have in common for sure is that they are your audience. If you're speaking to a group, they're sharing the same space and time, listening to your presentation in a room or auditorium. A comment about the weather or the acoustics is one way to bring them together and make them more responsive. In a printed document, chances are your audience is holding the piece in their hands and acknowledging that can create a connection. If your communication is electronic in nature, you can be sure your audience is looking at a screen. Find a way to bring that fact into your discussion. The important thing to remember is that people like to be treated as individuals, not as members of a group, and anything you can do to establish even a small sense of empathy and intimacy goes a long way toward getting the dopamine flowing and bringing your audience around to your side in that critical first Three Second Window. Conveying the idea that we're in this together is always compelling.

Once the If/Then list is complete, it's time to think about what you want your audience to do in response to your communication. It could be to take some action, such as making a purchase, or simply to show interest in some way. Don't take it for granted that everyone knows what your "call to action" is. Spell it out and be specific, ask them directly to do something and ask them several times. Using the real estate example, the call to action could be for the audience to request more information or a phone consultation about how Web tools can help them be more successful. Depending upon the circumstances, the call to action might be to make a trial purchase. Be sure to include *how* you want your audience to respond. Is the response path by phone or Web? Is it by snail mail or, in the case of a live presentation, to raise their hands and ask questions? Provide them with phone numbers, Web addresses, postal addresses or whatever information they need to get in touch. And remember, the more choices you give them, the more likely they are to respond.

The next part of the strategy is perhaps the most important. It has to do with spelling out the main thing you want your audience to get from your communication; let's call it the takeaway. Think of it this way: A member of your audience has just read your communication or finished listening to it in person. A friend asks, "So what was that all about?" The answer your audience member makes should be short and sweet, no more than one brief sentence long. Phrase your takeaway from an audience member's perspective. Use action words and stay away from passive words. Again, going back to the real estate example, a good takeaway might read something like this: "I should get Web tools for real estate agents because it will help me make more sales." Don't worry about phrasing the takeaway in the tone and manner of your communication. It's doubtful that the takeaway as expressed in the strategy will ever be stated quite that way in the actual communication. The takeaway is strictly for your use in crafting your communication in a way that will lead your audience to make their decision in your favor.

The final part of the strategy is the offer. The offer is simply something you will give your target audience for responding or making a purchase, a donation or whatever your call to action requires. Think of the offer as a sweetener. Chances are you've created a compelling argument for why your audience should respond, and you'll get a lot of people to do just that. But some will need a little more incentive. They might be interested, but need more convincing. An offer can give these fence sitters the push they need to take the plunge. You don't have to offer a lot. It could be something physical, such as a brochure with more information, a free white paper by an independent analyst, or a useful trinket of some kind. Or it could be an in-person, phone or Web consultation. We call these kinds of offers low-commitment offers because the target audience only has to ask to get them. The high-commitment offer, on the other hand, requires a purchase or some other investment to receive. You might offer a discount, a premium or an extra service, such as free shipping, when your prospect agrees to buy. Whatever your offer, it will work best to create that extra bit of desire if it is connected to the idea, product or service your communication is promoting. On the following pages, you can read an actual strategy our agency created for Cellular One.

Current Market Situation

Competition across the wireless industry is fierce, with the larger providers dominating the "Free Calling Network" landscape. The prospect of getting such a big free calling network poses a temptation for current Cellular One customers to jump ship. Cellular One, though, is able to compete very well with the big companies on value and "home town service".

To promote our value and service position, Cellular One has introduced a new campaign that focuses on our customer commitment. In addition, Cellular One has developed a customer segmentation model that enables us to target high-value customers with communications custom-tailored to their value.

The above factors make it the perfect time to reach out to our highest value customers with an excellent offer, introduce them to our new look and feel, and let them know how much we value their business.

Direct Marketing Goal

Generate a 12% conversion rate among Tier One and Tier Two customers.

Target Audience Description

Tier One and Tier Two Cellular One customers in "tender time" (out of contract or within 2 months of contract expiration).

Target Audience Assumptions and Implications

1. Target Audience is a Cellular One customer and has a positive image of us...
   Which means... we should remind them how much they like and rely upon their service.
2. Target Audience has not yet seen our new look and feel...

Which means… we need to explain that our new image represents our renewed commitment to their satisfaction.

3. Target Audience doesn't realize they are out of contract or very close to being out of contract and are free to switch without incurring a penalty… Which means… we should not mention this fact.

4. Target Audience has not received any customer appreciation communication from Cellular One before and doesn't feel valued… Which means… we should emphasize how much we really do value them as customers by spelling out the 4 points; Guaranteed Satisfaction, More Choices, Loyalty Rewarded, and You Matter.

5. Target Audience is using an old phone… Which means… we should point out the benefits of getting a new state-of-the-art phone.

6. Target Audience is tempted to switch to a provider with a larger mobile-to-mobile calling network… Which means… we need to emphasize that our network coverage is excellent and that our service and rate plans are designed to fit their lifestyle.

7. Target Audience gets a lot of wireless offers in the mail… Which means… we need to develop creative that makes a strong impact.

8. Target Audience is happy with their wireless service… Which means… we need to emphasize that while the look and feel of our company has changed a bit, their high-quality service is going to stay the same.

9. Target Audience will have a lot of information to digest from our mailing… Which means… we need to allow enough real estate to communicate our message.

10. Target Audience leads a busy life and won't want to spend a lot of their time reading a boring mail piece… Which means… we have to present the information in an entertaining and compelling way.

11. Target Audience is proud to live in a rural area… Which means… we should acknowledge that they inhabit the "wide open spaces" and emphasize that our company "lives" there too.

12. Target Audience sees a 2-year contract as protection for them… Which means… we should nurture that perception.

13. Target Audience gets a lot of value from their wireless service each month… Which means… we need to gently remind them what life would be like without their wireless phones.

14. Target Audience will be skeptical that we really see them as special and highly-valued… Which means… we will have to make it clear that our offer is only for certain customers like them.

Offer

Free LG 3200 phone, or Audiovox 8910 camera phone for 19.99, both with 2-year agreement.

Single Net Impression

"I should re-sign with Cellular One because they care enough about me to give me the best value and service".

Call To Action

Call right away and get a new phone.

Response Path

Call the 800 number

Mandatories

New brand look and feel
New logo and tag line
Hello2Fun logo
Legal copy

The "candy box" is The Big Idea that executed the strategy. It was the best of many ideas we came up with and motivated a lot of customers to stick with our client, Cellular One.

The Big Idea

Now that your strategy is complete, it's time to get to the really fun part: the creative. The creative is the execution of the strategy. It's what gives the strategy form and life and turns it into a Three Second Window; it's words and images blended to communicate a message that will create desire in a tightly defined group of people. To do this, you will need a concept or, as we call it at our agency, The Big Idea.

The Big Idea is a theme, concept or framework that can be used to entertain, inform and persuade. The Bible often uses parables to express some moral truth. In modern marketing-speak, we would call a parable a kind of concept. But how do you come up with a strong, original concept—one that will stimulate the reward system, get the dopamine flowing and create a meaningful Three Second Window?

When I was teaching introductory graphic design at Penn State, part of my job was to teach students how to generate good ideas. To do that, I required them to present ten ideas each studio session. There were two three-hour studios each week, which meant students had to come up with ten fresh ideas every two or three days. Now, the majority of my students at this level had never tried their hands at graphic design. They were not yet trained in the art of "concepting," and they found it very hard to do. I always gave them tight parameters, defined the challenge for them and essentially gave them a strategy from which to work. Still, coming up with ten ideas seemed to be beyond the ability of most new designers. I can't count the number of times a student would come to me with two or three sketches and say, "But I just can't think of any more ideas."

To help, I shared with them a trick I learned in my own early design education: "This is going to take a bit of self-discipline," I would say, "but believe me, if you will try it, it will help. Sit in front of your desk for one hour. Do not allow yourself to leave your chair, listen to music or the radio, watch TV or read. Eat and drink first, don't have any of that stuff around when you start to concept. Have only a pencil and paper, be alone in your room and don't speak to anyone. Think about that single point you are trying to communicate. Block everything else out, focus only on the task at hand."

I told them there was no requirement at this point to come up with any ideas. "Simply think about what you're trying to accomplish. Pretty soon, you'll start to doodle. You'll be producing ideas; don't worry if they're not good ideas, the important thing at this point is to exercise your creative muscles.

At first, the ideas will flow almost effortlessly, but soon they'll begin to dry up, and before long, you'll run completely out of ideas. You'll get frustrated, you'll think of a dozen other things you should be doing. You'll be tempted to get up and stretch, or get a drink, maybe catch up on your laundry. You'll be so frustrated from trying to come up with ideas that just about any other task will look good. Fight through it. Resist the temptation, because the really good stuff is about to happen. It's at this point in the creative process when the unexpected ideas spring into being, but you have to fight through that wall to where all the good, original ideas live."

I know not all students took my advice, because it showed in their work, or rather lack of work. I could spot immediately the ones who did, though, because their work improved dramatically.

The world is full of dull, predictable and boring ideas that are the product of *linear* thinking alone. An example of linear thinking is apparent in the equation 1 + 1 = 2. Pretty predictable, pretty uninspiring. The best ideas are the unexpected ones that are the product of *lateral* thinking. An example of lateral thinking is seen in the equation 1 + 1 = 487. There's an unanswered question in the second example that piques interest and invites further investigation. When your audience sees that equation, chances are they're going to be intrigued.

Those of us in the creative professions are no different than anyone else. We weren't born with the ability to come up with good, original ideas, we had to learn techniques that allow us to develop compelling concepts in a short time. We had to learn how to get in touch with our subconscious brains and stimulate our own reward systems so that we could stimulate the reward systems of our audiences. But while creative professionals are not necessarily genetically predisposed to being creative, they do learn to think about the world in a slightly different way—a skewed, or lateral, way. A lateral-thinking exercise I find particularly helpful is to think of an image or a phrase that has absolutely nothing to do with the communication problem I'm trying to solve. For a moment, I forget about my carefully crafted strategy and throw caution to the wind. I call this my "flaming orange" exercise. The name comes from an episode early in my design career when I was struggling with the design of a magazine cover for a story about the nation's economic health. Unable to come up with an original idea

I felt did the story justice, out of sheer frustration, I simply sketched an image that was completely unrelated to the story. It was a drawing of a hand holding an orange. Don't ask me why I came up with that particular image, it was just something that popped into my mind. Then I drew angry red flames coming up from the orange (maybe because I was a bit angry?). This image had nothing to do with the magazine story. It was completely out of left field, but it got me thinking. Just for fun, I tried to come up with a way to make the idea work. I made up stories about how a hand holding a flaming orange could express the health of an economy. Believe me, I came up with some pretty far-fetched, totally unworkable ideas, but as I sifted through the problem, my mind began to make connections that I normally wouldn't see through linear thinking. What if the hand wasn't holding an orange, but something else? I began to play with the idea. I omitted the orange and substituted a strip of electrocardiogram readout. I omitted the flames, but kept the red color. I inserted the color blue onto the white of the paper to make the color combination of the U.S. flag. The result was the trace of a heartbeat on a red, white and blue strip of EKG paper resembling the U.S. flag. In a short time, I had come up with an idea that communicated exactly what I wanted to say in a very original, eye-catching way. I remember my client's amazed expression upon seeing the magazine cover. "How in the world did you ever think of that?" he said.

"Oh," I shrugged, "it's just what I do."

The point of the flaming orange exercise is that it gives you an original place to start and in my experience, that is the best place to be.

The moral of this story is never to settle for your first idea. The trick to coming up with a really original idea is to come up with a lot of ideas and choose the best. And how do you know which idea is best? Easy—you've got your strategy to use as a yardstick. Which of your ideas best communicates the takeaway? Which one speaks to the target audience in a way that will resonate with them? Which of your many ideas best meets the situation statement? Which one passes the dopamine test and will create the most powerful Three Second Window?

Okay. The strategy is complete, and you have a solid blueprint for your communication. You've defined all the important parts, and you have a good concept. Now you can begin to tell your story. There's one important caveat, though, that you need to consider. Your concept needs to be original, but it also needs to be understandable to others and you will have to execute it in telling your story. I've seen some very nice ideas that would work in some media and not others. For instance, a concept that might be powerful as a TV spot might not work as a magazine ad. You will need to make those kinds of calls for yourself and there's really no substitute for experience. One thing I can tell you is that the simplest ideas are almost always the best—and the hardest to come up with. Don't make your concept so complicated that it takes half an hour for your target audience to figure out what you're trying to communicate. If your idea requires multiple images, lots of descriptors and combinations of constructs, similes and metaphors, you're probably looking at a dud.

Theme

All stories are the same at their most basic levels. Love, lust, desire, revenge, struggle, passion, triumph and every other theme you can think of spring from the same source: *the drive to survive*. Survival, after all, is the basic motivation behind all human behavior and it's the most powerful stimulator of the reward system. Today, few of us have to actually fight for our lives. Most of us live in comfortable homes, sheltered from the weather; our food sources are safe and readily available, and we have family and friends to help us celebrate in good times and commiserate with us in bad. So our survival instincts are directed in other ways—we fall in love and have children, we make friends, we talk to our neighbors over the backyard fence, we play and buy things and we eat and drink. Food and water are of course basic needs for day-to-day physical survival. Shelter we can do without a little longer, but in the end we need to get in out of the elements or perish. We need other like-minded people around us in the form of a community to help us secure food and shelter and we need sex to ensure the survival of our genes. The things we are most interested in are those things that provide us with survival advantages. They are the topics that stimulate the reward system to release dopamine and give us that good feeling that our human needs are being met. In the end, every good story, every Three Second Window, is a lesson about survival.

When we think of a story, we usually think of a narrative made up of words, either written or spoken. But there can be a lot more to storytelling than that. When I sit down to create an ad or some other communication, I think about the structure first, before I ever write a single word or create a drawing, photograph or other visual element.

I think back to Aristotle's triad: *the purpose of all communication is to entertain, to inform, to persuade.* The first thing I want to do is attract my target audience's attention. I know that the best way to do that is to create an emotional response—tickle their reward systems—so I try to create a beginning that will be entertaining. There's nothing revolutionary about this approach, but it is surprising how many ads, documents and presentations start in the middle of the story by asking you to buy something or believe this or that. Starting out by entertaining is the hallmark of all successful communication.

To Entertain

Think about how a favorite novel or movie begins. Sometimes it will start with a compelling Three Second Window: a car chase, a fistfight, a wedding or a courtroom or hospital scene. We put ourselves in the hero's position and we're immediately interested in how or if the protagonist will survive the struggle. What will be the outcome of the car chase? Who's going to win the fight? Will our hero prevail? What's in store for the wedding couple? Will they live long and prosper or will fate step in to stir things up? What is the crime, whom is the victim and what will happen to the perpetrator? Will the patient survive the surgery? In the end, our interest hinges on the survival of the protagonists, and boy, does the dopamine ever get flowing. Other times, great stories begin by focusing on an interesting character, and his or her actions or thoughts give us insight into the character's personality and motives. Still other stories begin by describing a setting. It might be the sea or the mountains, a city, a neighborhood, a house or a room. The setting could be a boat or a ship in space. However your favorite story begins, it will no doubt have one goal: to get you interested, to create an emotional hook that you can't resist.

You may not be writing a novel or a screenplay, but your communication should perform the same function. The beginning is the most important part of any story. It's the part of your communication that makes people want to go along with you and find out more. By entertaining your target audience, you are softening up their natural resistance to "being sold" on your message. There are lots of ways to do this, and the exact way you do it will depend upon the content of your message, the tone and manner and of course your skill as a storyteller. You might garner attention through the use of a bold statement, a provocative or controversial image or an incomplete, enigmatic or seemingly contradictory thought that requires further investigation by the target audience to resolve. But no matter what tack you take, remember that the more directly it relates to survival in an economic, physical, emotional or other way, the more power it will have to elicit a strong emotional response and the greater will be your chance for success.

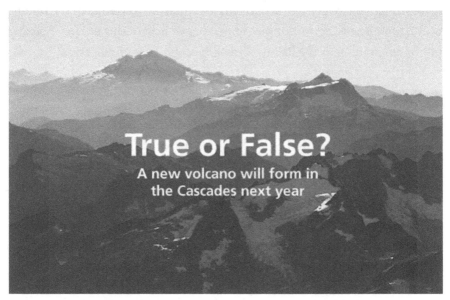

This ad my agency, Orbit Direct, created for a local Seattle newspaper poses the idea that a new volcano might erupt soon. With memories of Mt. St. Helens lingering, recipients were eager to find out if there is indeed a survival threat lurking.

To Inform

Now that you've got your target audience warmed up and have the dopamine flowing, explain why it's important for them to delve deeper into your message. They are going to want to know *What's In It For Me,* or *WIIFM.* Explain the benefit your target audience can expect. Make it personal, showing how what you have to say will make life better, safer, happier. If it's a business communication, how can you help your target audience be more successful?

It's important to frame this part of your message in terms of survival, too, whether economic, emotional, social or in some cases even physical, because remember that you're not talking to the conscious mind at this point, you're getting in touch with the subconscious reward system. You're creating a Three Second Window, which is, after all, where all the decisions really get made.

People need and expect continuity, so make the transition from the entertainment part of your story to the information part smooth. Pay off the initial thought through words and images, but avoid being too obvious or heavy-handed. Too often we see copy that simply labels or restates an image in words. The image and words should add meaning to each other and make the combination even more compelling. A good way to tell if you have created a compelling word/image combination is to perform this simple test: If the photo or the copy can stand alone and convey a complete, compelling thought, you're probably not there yet. An ideal situation occurs when the image needs the words to make a complete thought and vice versa. A colleague of mine at Penn State, Lanny Sommese, had a nice way of phrasing it. He would often talk about the symbiotic relationship between words and pictures as *visual/verbal closure*. What he meant was that the image and words have to be present to communicate a coherent thought, that they complement and complete—not simply describe—each other.

Inside, this "Volcano" mailer paid off the headline with a whimsical note and prompted the reader to respond to learn the answer to the question posed by the cover.

Connect the benefit, or WIIFM, to the opening in a way that is natural. You want to leverage the interest you have created to carry over to the benefit you are offering. Focus on the main benefit you determined to be most important when you created your strategy. This is the meat of the message and the part that will do the most to stimulate the reward system. Frame it as a survival benefit and state it clearly and in plain language. Use words and images to create visual/verbal closure to reinforce the benefit in more than one way. You want to appeal to the emotions you've started bubbling toward the surface, but be sure to provide food for thought, too. It's time to buttress your benefit with support points that speak to reason as well. These support points usually take the form either of other benefits or of features with associated benefits.

To Persuade

No one likes to be pressured, which is why the art of persuasion is best practiced gently. Persuasion is something you need to build up to in your communication. Maybe that's why it's the last item on Aristotle's list.

Assuming the first two parts of your communication have done their jobs to entertain and inform, persuading your target audience should fall naturally into the flow of your communication. In fact, the audience should, at this point, be eager to do what you want them to, but you'll still need to buttress the emotional responses you've created with reason. Refer back to the emotional arguments you made earlier and give tangible support points. Illustrate the benefits and attach them to features. Remind your audience why they need or want what you have to offer, and ask them for a response. Often in the persuasion phase of a communication, it's a good idea to involve the audience by asking questions— and providing the answers. You might suggest they imagine how their lives will be impacted by responding to your call to action. If you're proposing a product or service whose primary benefit is saving money, for instance, you might create a chart that shows your target audience's expenses before and after purchasing your product or service. Be sure to do the math for them so that they can see in real terms the benefits you are proposing.

For the sake of illustration, I've broken down Aristotle's three purposes of communication—to entertain, to inform and to persuade—into distinct parts.

In reality, no such clear distinction exists, or at least it shouldn't. The purposes overlap and intertwine. Your communication should be informing and persuading from the start, and it should always be entertaining. But it's important to remember that there needs to be focus on each purpose in its appropriate place and time. There's no hard-and-fast rule about how to accomplish this. But once you have Aristotle's structure in mind, you'll discover original, compelling and fun ways that will create surprising and delightful Three Second Windows for you and your audience. And after all, isn't that what it's about?

The Buying Cycle

It's important to remember to speak *to* your audience, not *at* them. Earlier in this chapter, we explored the demographics of an audience—statistics such as age, income, gender and marital status. Another important characteristic that warrants attention is where your audience is in The Buying Cycle. At my agency, we use The Buying Cycle on every project because it helps us speak to our audience as individuals. It helps us target our message more tightly, and boy, does it work.

Here's an example of how The Buying Cycle can help you create successful communication: I was working for one of Apple Computer's ad agencies back when Microsoft first introduced Windows. It was the early nineties, and the marketing people at Apple were more than a little worried that Microsoft's entry into the graphical user interface market would take a big chunk out of the Apple business. We were put to work coming up with ways to counteract Windows. I remember traveling from the Seattle agency to Apple's headquarters in Cupertino, California, to show our concepts to their marketing people. We assembled in a conference room with a group of very frustrated-looking Apple execs. The atmosphere was charged with tension, my writing partner and I traded glances, and he whispered to me, "This could get ugly…"

Today, Apple "owns" the higher education market. Macs can be found in almost every university department, and that's no accident. It's been a long-standing Apple marketing strategy to get young people hooked on the Mac at an early, formative age, so Apple gives academics special attention. But back in the early nineties, this approach was just taking shape. My creative partner and I had been given the task of creating advertising that would counteract the appeal of Windows to the academic market. After all, if a Windows machine did basically the same thing as a Mac and cost less, why not go for the cheaper machine? This of course wasn't true—the Windows interface was comparatively clunky, unreliable and no match for the Mac—but the marketing people at Apple felt sure this was the story Microsoft would try to sell. It was the kind of thinking that was keeping Apple execs up at night and they were looking to us for an answer.

We were well aware of the issues Apple was facing, and we'd come up with some great ideas we felt sure would go a long way toward supporting the Mac in the colleges and universities. But we knew from past experience that when clients are scared, they are very hard to please. So not only did we need to produce killer creative, but we also had to provide a bulletproof argument for why it would work. So before we showed our creative ideas, we laid the groundwork by introducing the Apple execs to The Buying Cycle. The Buying Cycle provides a way to create advertising that will work for any given target audience.

Back at Apple, the room was settling down. The usual posturing and small talk subsided and my writing partner and I took the floor. We began by outlining the general situation between Apple and Windows, then turned the discussion toward the target audience: college and university professors. We introduced the idea behind The Buying Cycle model by explaining that all buyers go through a series of steps when they make a purchase. They move from step one to step two and so on. To further illustrate The Buying Cycle, we wrote "AIRDU" on the whiteboard, which stands for:

- Awareness
- Interest
- Research
- Decision to Buy
- Use Exclusively

These, according to The Buying Cycle model, are the stages each one of us goes through when making a purchase decision. We explained that our audience of academics was already at the Awareness stage, that is, they knew who Apple was. They had high brand awareness, were familiar with the graphical user interface and had a generally positive view of Apple. That meant we didn't have to waste words and space in the ad to introduce the Mac, telling them something they already knew. This explanation brought an affirmative murmur and nodding of heads. My writing partner and I started to feel a little better. Next, we made the point that since our target audience was always interested in upgrading and adding to the technical capabilities of their departments, we could safely assume that they were at least interested in getting a new computer or, better yet, a bunch of new computers for their departments. This placed them firmly in the Interest stage. Again, our words were greeted with an appreciative response from the Apple people. I glanced at my writing partner. Was that a smile starting to form on his lips? So, we reasoned, according to The Buying Cycle model, the goal of our ad should be to move our audience from the Interest stage to the Research stage. Our objective, we explained, was to get our target audience to compare the Mac to Windows, in other words, to perform research. To help them do this, our ad would provide a framework of features and benefits, heavily weighted in the Mac's favor, of course, that would move them to the next stage, Decision to Buy. The room was silent for a few moments. We looked around at the dozen or so faces, then broad smiles and enthusiastic conversation broke out. We had them in the palms of our hands. The creative we showed met with instant approval, all because we had set the stage so that no other approach would seem reasonable. Oh, and by the way, the ad was a great success and made a lot of sales. It didn't hurt our careers, either.

Today, The Buying Cycle is an important part of every ad we produce at our agency. It gives a grounding in reality that helps clients understand the reasoning behind the words and pictures and provides a yardstick with which to measure how well an ad will resonate with a given target audience. But it's not just for producing mass communication. You can use The Buying Cycle, too, in a less formal way to get your point across, whether it's to a group of a hundred people or one on one. Simply establish what stage of The Buying Cycle your target audience is in. Do they know you or the product or service you are promoting? If not, you'd better spend some time on an introduction. You need to establish that your product or service is reliable, is stable and does what you claim. Awareness and a positive image are the foundation upon which all arguments must be based to be effective. Establish your credibility from the get-go so that what you say and do will carry more weight. Take the time to make clear your bona fides: Think of possible issues that might arise in your target audience's minds, raise them early and knock them down with reason and emotion. Once you've built your foundation of trust, you can move your audience to the next stage, Interest. Explain why your product or service is valuable to them, how they can benefit and why. Provide concrete examples and even use testimonials and anecdotes to illustrate. Get them interested in what you have to say by explaining how your product or service can make their lives better, easier and more enjoyable. Now that they're interested, invite comparison with competitors or life without all the benefits you can provide. Move them to the Research stage but don't try to sell them yet, go point by point, making clear, concise arguments, and remember to ask questions. "Is that something you would find valuable? Is there a particular problem that you need help with?" Involving your target audience in the process helps you understand where they are and where you need to help them be.

The Buying Cycle Stages	Audience State of Mind
Awareness	"I know who you are."
Interest	"I might use your product."
Research	"I will look at your product."
Decision to Buy	"I'll make a trial purchase."
Use Exclusively	"I'll only buy from you."

Once you've moved your target audience to the Research stage, have gotten them to make comparisons and see that what you're offering is superior, it's time to ask for the sale, that is, move them to the Decision to Buy stage. You've built a bulletproof argument in your favor, one that any reasonable person will find hard to resist, and if you've done a good job in the preceding stages, this should be the easiest one of all. The next stage, Use Exclusively, is where your customers become evangelists for you, your product or service. You have so pleased them that they tell their friends, which generates additional converts to your brand.

Now, I've greatly compressed the process and placed it in a commercial, face-to-face situation for purposes of illustration. Different people and purchase decisions move through The Buying Cycle at different rates. Some even skip stages, but the model is useful in almost every situation and, with a little imagination and ingenuity, you can find your own ways of adapting The Buying Cycle to unlock and awaken your own creative impulses, create compelling Three Second Windows that get the dopamine flowing and achieve your business and personal goals.

Chapter 8

The Power of Three

It's been said that brevity is the soul of wit. Brevity is also important in every other kind of communication. Once upon a time, before the widespread use of computers and writing and graphics programs, creating visual and written communication was left to the professional copywriters and graphic designers. Professionals in these fields are trained to create Three Second Windows that focus on the points they are trying to make, pare down and eliminate the superfluous and organize information in ways that make sense to the reader. Today, most people are able to access the tools of the professional writer and designer but lack the training to use them in the most effective way. We've all seen the results. Who hasn't had to wade through reports filled with words, pictures and diagrams that seem to have no beginning and no end—and no point? Or suffer through long, unorganized presentations? Bad communication is worse than no communication at all. On the other hand, effective communication in the world of business is the path to success.

I used to work with a fellow who was infamous around the agency for creating presentations that put people to sleep. He subscribed to the notion that *more is more*. He was notorious for producing long, meandering, tedious and mind-numbingly boring documents and PowerPoint presentations. Clients would invariably plead, about forty minutes into one of his torture sessions, "Could you please just get to the point?" This poor guy, we'll call him Joe, would hem and haw and befuddle his audience with a series of non sequiturs, usually with the result that our client would give up trying to get an answer and just suffer the remainder of Joe's presentation in painful silence. It was an awful thing to watch. Many times I tried to dissuade Joe from his practice of pointless marathon presentations but to no avail. He was completely immune to even the most straightforward critique and insisted on continuing his self-defeating practice. I think Joe is driving a cab today.

Joe's problem was that he was unable to organize his thoughts in a way that made them accessible to other people (he refused to build his presentations on a well-thought out strategy). He didn't understand that information has to be broken down into digestible chunks: small bits that when combined complete a thought. Joe just didn't recognize the power of three.

Why three? Three is a very interesting number with unique properties. Three is the number of primary colors: red, blue and yellow. Three is the number of the basic shapes: square, circle and triangle. Three is the number of sides of a triangle, which is the strongest structural form. And three is also the largest number of items we humans can easily visualize. I know that last one sounds a bit cockeyed, so let me present you with a simple exercise to support my point:

Close your eyes and visualize in your mind's eye a single black dot. Pretty easy, right? Now, add another dot just like it. How did you arrange the dots? Side by side or one on top of the other? Maybe you organized them diagonally. However you put them together, you probably didn't have much trouble creating the pair. You can easily imagine those two dots and recognize them as a group of two. You don't have to count or even look very hard. A quick glance will do. Now, add another identical dot. How did you create that grouping? In a horizontal or vertical row? Maybe as a triangle. However you arranged them, it's still pretty easy to recognize the grouping of three at a glance. Now add one more dot to make a total of four. This grouping is still easily recognizable but perhaps not quite as quickly as the group of three is. Okay, please bear with me. Add one more dot to make five. Now it's getting pretty complicated. You probably have to count or break down the group of five into one group of three and another group of two. Once you get to six or seven, it becomes very hard to create easily recognizable groupings. It seems that three is about the highest number most of us can recognize without having to count or think about it.

Not only does it seem that three is the highest grouping we can easily and quickly recognize, but there's also something satisfying about the number three. It has a kind of harmony and stability about it, and not just visually. We humans also seem to like the number three when it comes to ideas. Take the Declaration of Independence, for example. It recognizes three inalienable rights: life, liberty and the pursuit of happiness. In the United States Constitution, our founding fathers thought it fit to organize the government into three branches, the legislative, executive and judicial. And the largest Christian denomination, the Catholic Church, even sees God in the number three: the Father, the Son, and the Holy Spirit.

To show the power of three, let's see how the examples I just mentioned might be grouped to make an impact you will easily remember:

- Life, Liberty and the Pursuit of Happiness
- Legislative, Executive, and Judicial
- The Father, the Son and the Holy Spirit

See how neat that works? Still, there's nothing magic about the number three; it just seems to work well for organizing things and ideas. It has a power to communicate in a way that other groupings lack. It seems to have the ability to produce dopamine at a greater rate than other numbers. Don't ask me why, it just does.

Use the power of three when you create a presentation or a document that others will have to view or read. Have a single major point and group your support points into sets of threes. Find as many ways to link the three support points as you can: through the use of similar sounding words, visually with graphic elements, through the benefits each point bestows and of course through their relationship to and support of your major point.

Meta-Language

When my daughter was struggling with her high school French class, she said to me one day, only half kidding, "Dad, those French have a word for everything!" Behind this seemingly inane remark is a basic truth about the world we live in.

It's a world of language. We think of ourselves and our surroundings in terms of words and pictures and we communicate with each other in the same way. We live inside language and are limited by the boundaries of language. What my daughter was trying to get at is that French has words for concepts that don't exist in English, and vice versa. Learning new concepts along with a new language can be very frustrating. It's a little like trying to imagine a color you've never seen.

Philosophers going back to Plato and Aristotle recognized this inherent problem with language and proposed methods for dealing with it. Later, around the turn of the nineteenth century, Ferdinand de Saussure, considered the father of modern linguistics, came up with new ways to think about how we communicate, which he dubbed *semiologie*. In the twentieth century, linguists such as Roland Barthes and Umberto Eco were instrumental in developing the system even further. Today, semiotics—a theory of signs and symbols—is taught in universities, colleges and art and design schools as a way to use both verbal and visual language more effectively, creatively and persuasively.

The Sign Function

Semiotics is simple and useful. Once you learn to think in a semiotic frame of mind, you'll look at communication in a very different way. Using language precisely and effectively is tough. It's often hard to find just the right words, and just as hard to figure out which images need to go where and why. Semiotics simplifies all that. It gives you a means to clarify what you want to say and to organize the verbal and visual information to help you make your point quickly, efficiently and in an engaging way.

There are a few basic concepts that you'll have to master, but with a little thought, they should come fairly easily. Semiotics begins with the idea of the sign function. The sign function is simply the act of communicating something to someone in some way. Think of the sign function not as a *thing*, such as a report or a presentation, but rather as a relationship between three parts:

- The object
- The audience
- The sign

In semiotics, none of these three parts stands alone. In order for one to exist, the other two must be present. Let's take a very simple example of the sign function and break it down to its three parts. Imagine you are driving down the street and you are pulled over by a police officer for speeding. You have a driver's license but it rests hidden and unseen in your wallet. No sign function has yet occurred. There is no object, no audience and no sign, at least not yet. You automatically reach into your wallet and take out your driver's license and hand it to the officer. He looks at it, checks that it's valid and hands it back. Bingo! A semiotic sign function has just occurred. All three parts were present.

What was the object? Who was the audience? What was the sign?

You might think the object was the driver's license itself, but it wasn't. The object in this case wasn't a physical thing at all: It was the permission granted to you by the state to operate a motor vehicle.

The audience was the police officer who pulled you over for going thirty-five in a twenty-miles-per-hour zone.

The sign is the driver's license itself, the actual thing that stands for the object.

A driver's license can create a sign function. It communicates
something (permission to drive) to someone (the police officer)
through a physical object (the driver's license itself).

Together, they communicate something (the object; permission to drive) to someone (the audience; the police officer) in some physical way (the sign; your driver's license). Put them together and you have a sign function.

The Sign

The sign is the physical representation of the object. It's the thing that stands for something else. The object in the example above is permission to drive: a concept. The object can also be something physical, such as a person or a book, or it can be an idea, such as freedom or oppression. It can also be an act, such as entrance or exit.

Let's think about the sign (your driver's license) for a moment. The sign is rarely a single thing. It's usually made up of lots of parts. In the case of your driver's license, it's probably made up of your picture, your name, your signature, maybe your fingerprint, your date of birth, an expiration date, and the state seal, plus a lot of colors, type, some paper and plastic and other official marks. In semiotics, each of these parts falls into one of three categories:

- A symbol
- An icon
- An index

Let's take the symbol first. You're no doubt familiar with symbols. They're everywhere. The U.S. flag is a symbol, the logo on your car is a symbol, a family crest is a symbol. But when we talk about the symbol in a semiotic context, we have to define the meaning a little more than that. In semiotics, the symbol is a freely created representation of some object. It's called a symbol because it has no natural connection to the thing it stands for. For instance, the letters you are reading on this page are all symbols, which make up words, which are symbols, too. Take the letter B, for example. The sound we think of when we think of the letter B is a sound we've been taught to associate with that particular shape, even though the shape in no way suggests any sound at all. All letters and words are symbols, but there are many other symbols, too. Let's take another look at your driver's license, because it's loaded with symbols. It probably contains a state seal, lots of type and of course your signature. All these are symbols because they have no natural relation to the things they represent, and they represent their objects only because we've all collectively agreed that they do. You're probably not used to thinking of your signature as a symbol, but in semiotics, it most definitely is.

Icons, on the other hand, have a natural connection to the object for which they stand. Take another look at your driver's license. Now look at your photograph. That's an icon because it looks like you. There might be an outline of your state, too. That's an icon because it bears a physical resemblance to the actual shape of your state. Icons differ from symbols because they *look like* the things they represent. Today we might think of icons in relation to computers, as those little pictures that resemble trashcans, clocks or pointing fingers.

The index, which is very different from the symbol and the icon, takes a little more head scratching to understand. The index uses an imprint or fragment of the object. For instance, footprints in the snow could be an index of the passage of an animal. Smoke on the horizon could be indexical of a house fire several miles away. An index is the indication of something that has happened. If your fingerprint is on your driver's license, that's an indexical representation of *you having placed your ink-coated finger on a piece of paper*. An index doesn't look like the thing it stands for in the way an icon does, nor is it a freely created representation, like a symbol. Instead, it represents its object through a natural physical connection but is not a physical likeness. For this reason, an indexical representation might be the strongest of the three. That's because indexical signs don't change from culture to culture, the way symbols do, nor are they affected by the passage of time, the way the iconic appearance of a person, place or thing might be.

By now I'm sure you've come up with many examples of your own, and you've probably noticed that there are signs that use one, two or all three types of representation. You've no doubt also noticed that the lines between the three types are often blurred. It's common to see signs that fuse the indexical and symbolic or the iconic and indexical or are a combination of all three. Take a moment to think about an ad, a book or a movie that you found entertaining or persuasive. Now think about it in terms of the three types of representation and try to see which dominated. Which was most powerful: a symbol, an icon or an index?

Semiotic Forms of Representation

Symbolic

Iconic

Indexical

Look closely at your driver's license. Can you pick out
which parts are symbols, icons or indices?

When you begin to look at things from a semiotic viewpoint, you are extending your thinking beyond the limitations of language. You are understanding how the different parts of a communication can be made to work together to create a more entertaining, interesting and persuasive Three Second Window.

It's important to remember that your audience isn't interested in *everything* you know, only in what you know that's relevant to their needs. Professional writers and designers understand this. When tackling a project, they amass much more information than they include in their final work. The trick is to know what to leave in and what to take out. A painting teacher I had in art school once told me the secret to creating great art is knowing when to stop. Deciding what to include and what to leave out is not easy, but semiotics offers a process that can help a lot. In semiotics, three operations can be performed when creating a sign to make it a briefer, more to the point and more powerful Three Second Window. They are:

- Insertion

- Omission

- Substitution

The sign goes through a lot of tweaking, or operations, before it is finished. We can think of those operations as adding to (insertion), taking away from (omission) and replacing (substitution). Think of it this way: You are preparing a presentation for work or school. You have gathered together facts, figures, charts, graphs and photos and combined all these parts in your presentation in rough form. You might have a photograph (an icon) that's meant to represent something (an object). Perhaps you insert another photo to complement and bring new meaning to the first. Maybe you take the photo out entirely. Is the presentation stronger without it? Perform a dopamine test to see. Perhaps you can substitute a symbol such as a flag or a logo. What happens when you try a different type of representation, such as an index? Remember that the sign function works as a relationship between the object, the audience and the sign.

Now that you've got an idea of what the sign function is and the parts that make it up, it's valuable to understand its three characteristics:

- Form

- Function

- Meaning

Let's use the traffic stop described earlier in this chapter as an example of a sign function, and let's say we want to turn that sign function into a televised public service announcement. The form of this particular sign function would be a short film using sound and moving images. The function could be to discourage speeding. The meaning might be that speeding is expensive.

We could change the form from a TV spot with sound and motion to a magazine ad or a billboard or poster. The audience could be teenage drivers watching MTV, or we could change the audience to people renewing their driver's licenses at the Department of Motor Vehicles. The meaning could change from "speeding is expensive" to "speeding is dangerous." The function might change from discouraging speeding to encouraging respect for the law. As you can see, each part and characteristic of the sign function affects every other part and characteristic.

I once designed a poster for a summer classical music festival called, "Music at Penn's Woods". I wanted the poster to be visually rich, so I employed all three forms of representation to communicate my message. I used a section of sheet music as the symbolic form. A photo of a blue summer sky with fluffy white clouds was the iconic form, and the shadow of a leaf was the indexical form. The result was a powerful sign function that garnered a lot of attention, filled up the festival seats and won several design awards.

Looking at every communication from a semiotic viewpoint helps you understand how to assemble the message in a way that successfully achieves your communication goals in the shortest way possible. What kind of sign will resonate best with your audience? Will they respond to one type of representation better than another? What form best serves your function and meaning? By understanding how different semiotic elements work together, you are able to use them as building blocks to create a Three Second Window that is more focused and gets your point across quicker and stronger.

The Medium Is the Message

At our agency, we have a saying: "Get them with paper, keep them with electrons." What that refers to is a strategy of acquiring new customers using ads sent through the mail. We've found that paper ads work a lot better at getting people to pay attention initially, while online communications are a more cost-effective way of maintaining the relationship once it's established. Ads that come in the mail, what we call direct mail, are the best way to introduce a company, a brand or a new product. That's because the medium, in this case paper, has as much to do with the effectiveness of the communication as do the words and pictures printed on it. If you want to communicate a message about high quality, you can use fine paper that conveys a sense of elegance, technical acumen or exclusivity. If you want to communicate thrift, practicality or concern for the environment, rough newsprint, raw cardboard or watermarked recycled papers are available to drive those points home. There are many types of paper, and each kind makes a statement. We use everything from fine laid linen to heavy, glossy cardboard to help communicate our clients' messages. In addition, how the paper is folded or cut can also add pizzazz to any message. By mating the message to the medium, you reinforce what is being conveyed by words and pictures. This means you can be briefer and more succinct, because all elements of your communication are driving home the same point.

We made this envelope out of paper called vellum. It's translucent (almost transparent, but not quite) to tease recipients about the contents.

Inside, the recipient found three cardboard pieces, each with a brief sales message, that could be assembled in several configurations. This desk toy mated the medium (interlocking puzzle pieces printed on heavy stock with photos of people) to the message: Come together with your friends and family with Cellular One. Because the medium helped communicate the message, the copy could be briefer and more to the point, increasing its effectiveness.

The idea of melding the medium with the message isn't a new one. Dutch painter Theo van Doesburg first discussed "concrete art" in his book *Manifesto of Concrete Art* in 1930. Van Doesburg wasn't talking about garden statuary; he and his fellow abstractionists, including Wassily Kandinsky and Max Bill, were discovering a new way to look at the world. These forward-thinking artists believed that art didn't have to be representative, that is, a line didn't have to stand for anything except a line. Color didn't have to be used only to represent a flower or a sunset; a block of color could simply be a block of color. These artists understood that enjoyment and insight into the human experience could be had from simple visual stimulation alone. They used color and line to create compositions that conveyed strictly abstract themes: motion, harmony, order and disorder. Later, out of this movement grew a smaller movement: concrete books. I first heard of concrete books in graduate school, where I learned how to express meaning through the conscious selection and manipulation of materials such as paper, wood, fabric, metal and found objects. In our studio, we would make books from different materials and use novel methods of construction. Although the books we students created were very different, they all shared one aspect: They all expressed content through form. I remember one book a fellow student did on the subject of frustration. She glued all the pages together so that to read her book, you had to actually tear it apart, piece by maddening piece. Talk about form merging with content. The course in concrete books was one of my favorite and most eye-opening classes, and I very successfully incorporated the concept of concrete art into my later work in advertising and design. It just goes to show how fine art can be translated into a viable tool of mass communication.

When Less Really Is More

To use media in ways that help communicate, it's necessary to first evaluate and understand the strengths and weaknesses of the medium under consideration. In other words, to find ways to meld form with content to make the message concrete. When I say that we get customers with paper and keep them with electrons, I mean that we make the initial contact usually by mailing an ad, then follow up with e-mail messages. We take this approach to exploit each medium's advantages while minimizing the negatives.

Every medium has its own characteristics: unique qualities that can be used to stimulate the reward system, create a powerful Three Second Window and emphasize the main message. For instance, paper is dimensional, tactile and highly portable and can be made interactive, too, but postage and printing are expensive. You can pin an interesting ad up on a bulletin board or attach it to your refrigerator door with magnets. The ad can even be the magnet itself. TV ads use motion and sound and are attention getting, but are difficult to target, plus producing and broadcasting a high-quality spot is expensive. The Web and e-mail are highly interactive and targetable, but in the end, they're only dots on a screen—not something you can easily hold in your hand. From my experience, few Web designers have yet to acknowledge this drawback, and so sites that are cluttered and really don't work very well are still being created. I have a theory as to why this is so and what to do about it.

Way back in the late twentieth century, when the Internet was just catching on, HTML programmers were about the only people creating Web sites. The tech guys were handy at writing code, but very few had any design training. The technical capabilities of the Web were extremely limited, which severely restricted the look. Many monitors were of low resolution and lacked the ability to reproduce anything except black and white and a few crude shades of gray. So those early, well-meaning and ambitious HTML programmers created their Web sites based on what they could do technically, which wasn't much.

As the Internet evolved and it became possible to be a bit more creative, the programmers adopted a "more is better" approach to Web design. You know what I'm talking about: Web sites that are cluttered with a hopelessly confusing conglomeration of buttons, pictures, flashing lights and whirling thingamajigs. It's a technologically advanced but aesthetically pedestrian look. The problem is, those HTML programmers broke all the rules of good design without knowing the rules in the first place. Their designs were based on the limitations and possibilities of machines, not on the needs of people. Rules are not sacred, but they do have value. There's nothing wrong with breaking the rules, *as long as you learn them first* (and we'll do just that in Chapter 9).

Communication is neither technology nor science. It's art, and every artistic endeavor has its rules, which are necessary to guide us through a process and arrive at a successful outcome. The rules of design are based in principles and take many forms. Rules might vary as the medium changes, but the principles remain valid. For instance, the rule for the size of type in a brochure is different than the rule for the size of type on a billboard, but the principle that *type needs to be easily legible* is the same.

The principles behind the design of a Web site and the design of a brochure or a book or, for that matter, a building, are identical. The same elements are present and the degree of aesthetic pleasure—and therefore functionality—depends on how well those principles are understood and how adroitly the elements are employed within a particular medium. A Web site transmitted by pixels on a screen has a different set of restrictions than does a brochure printed in ink on paper. Still, there's no reason that the Web site can't function as a Web site and still meet the human need for aesthetic fulfillment. After all, our hardwired aesthetic preferences don't change when we go from words and pictures on paper to words and pictures projected onto an electronic screen. In his book *A Primer of Visual Literacy*, Donis A. Dondis writes that "the American architect Sullivan's dictum 'form follows function' is most dynamically illustrated by the airplane designer, whose own preferences are limited by what assembled shapes, proportions, and materials will, in fact, really fly. The final product is shaped by what it does. But in the subtler problems of design there are many products that can reflect the subjective tastes of the designer and still function perfectly well." I suggest this corollary: *every product, including Web sites, must meet the aesthetic needs of the user to function well.*

I read somewhere that it takes only one-twentieth of a second for a person to decide whether he or she likes the look of a Web site. I'm willing to bet that it takes about the same amount of time for a person to decide whether he or she likes the look of *anything*, be it a Web site, a book cover, a house, a car or another person. As we've seen from previous chapters, the subconscious is very fast at making those kinds of decisions.

According to Netcraft, an online company that keeps track of such things, there are over one hundred million Web sites in the world as of this writing, with over three million new sites being added each month. Most Web sites I see still cling to the old anti-aesthetic approach practiced by early programmers: lots of clutter, no clear sense of hierarchy, bad composition, poor practice of typography and the usual collection of bells and whistles that tend to create a sense of frustration rather than one of aesthetic pleasure. It's no surprise that the effectiveness of these poorly designed sites is steadily declining. The number of people who go beyond the first page of a Web site is fewer with every passing day. Certainly some of this failure is due to a phenomenon known as the adoption curve, which describes the human tendency to tire of familiar activities such as clicking on banner ads. Once the newness has worn off, fewer people will repeat the experience. Poor design only exacerbates the problem. Another reason many Web sites don't work well is that "data experts" often override the recommendations of the creative folk. I was present at a lecture given by one such expert, who proudly proclaimed that she had arrived at over a thousand statistically valid compositions that, when implemented by the designers, would improve the effectiveness of her company's Web site by some remarkable percentage point. She believed she had arrived at the perfect Web site design, the perfect Three Second Window, through a mathematical equation!

There are, however, Web sites that work really well. I spoke with my friend Sharon Long Baerny about this very thing. She is the principal of a company called We Know Words and is involved in all aspects of Web and e-mail marketing and copywriting, including how to get her clients' sites to pop up first in a Google search. When I asked her about the decline in effectiveness of the Web, she told me there are several reasons. "People will find your site on a search engine, such as Google, then try to figure out as quickly as they can if it has the content they are looking for. If the home page is confusing, if there's too much clutter and junk, they'll skip right past and go to the next listing. There are so many Web sites out there, people just aren't willing to invest time trying to decipher a confusing home page."

"The Web sites that work really well are the ones that provide a clear focal point that communicates quickly what the reader can expect content-wise."

I asked Sharon about the way most Web sites are written and she became very animated. "That's one of the things that really bugs me. Most of the Web sites you see today are all about the company. They want to tell you their life story, no detail is too insignificant. What they should really be writing about is how they can help the reader. The copy should be client-centric. People care about what the company can do for them, not about the company. Once you've communicated that, you've pretty much got their attention and they'll stick around. Then you can give readers the option to learn more about who and what the company is and does."

How do good Web sites get us to stop, pay attention and search for meaning? Mark Wyner is one of the few Web designers who knows how to create a site that is highly functional by being pleasing to the eye. When I spoke with Mark about his philosophy, he had a lot to say. "Computers and computer screens are basically kind of off-putting, they're not all that friendly. When I design a Web site, I try to give it a sense of humanity, I try to make people forget they're staring at a computer screen. The screen is a very inorganic thing, and I think people really prefer a more organic experience. That's one of the reasons I usually include a nature-related photo, you know, something pleasant for the eye to rest on."

What Mark is talking about is one of the very basic principles of design that every first-quarter design student learns early on, but that most Web designers never catch on to: Aesthetic pleasure is the first function of any visual design, whether it's on paper or an electronic screen. The first and most important thing is to gain people's attention, to create a powerful Three Second Window, and get the reward system to respond with that shot of dopamine. "People tend to surf off your page pretty quickly if you don't give them a reason to linger," Mark says. "Think of the home page as the lobby of your office or your front room; make it warm, human and inviting. Sure, information is important, but unless it's presented in a way that's clear and pleasing to the eye, you're not going to get people to hang around."

Mark Wyner is a sought-after Web designer with many years of experience. He knows the principles of design and he uses them to create highly effective sites for his clients. Mastering graphic design is a lifelong pursuit and even those students who have completed a four or five-year course of study are still novices. I have been a designer for more than thirty years and I'm still learning. Although presenting a graphic design curriculum is outside the scope of this book, just knowing certain design principles and concepts and acquiring a design vocabulary will prove very helpful in communicating with the "creative types" in your life and in developing your own successful communications. From the layout of a business letter to your resume, from presentations to Web sites, once you learn the rules, you can experiment with them, push the boundaries and find new and interesting ways to express yourself and create your own brand of success.

This home page designed by Mark Wyner exhibits the principles of good design. With a few minor changes, it would work equally well as a brochure or print ad.

If I had to make a blanket statement about how to create successful communications, I'd say, "First, keep it simple." Don't be afraid of white space, but instead use it to direct the eye to the most important thing on the page or screen. Make a list of the three most important points you want to make and rank them. Make the number-one point most prominent. Position the word or picture so that it is the first thing the eye goes to. I know what you're thinking: "How do I know where a person's eye is going to go to first?" That's one of those questions researchers have tried to answer for a long time, and there is a ton of theories about it. I've seen eye-tracking studies that say one thing, while other eye-tracking studies say the opposite. The truth is, you, as the designer, decide where your viewer's eye will go first by the way you construct your composition. If you place a picture or a word off by itself in any corner, the eye will go there first. In all my years as a graphic designer, I've never seen any credible evidence that there is an inherent place on the page or screen that automatically draws the eye regardless of whatever else is present.

The principles of art and design have been around for as long as we've been human. The rules derived from eye-tracking studies have not. When we talk about breaking the rules, what we really mean is finding new ways to apply the principles behind them. Each of us has the ability to see in new and interesting ways, and learning a few basic principles of visual aesthetics will take you a long way toward simplifying your message and creating success in all your business communications.

Chapter 9

Picasso's Napkin

The story goes that the artist, Pablo Picasso, was having dinner in a restaurant one evening when a woman approached him. She introduced herself, told the master how much she cherished his work and asked shyly if he would sketch a little something on her napkin. Picasso took a pen from his pocket and in a few seconds produced a small drawing. Handing the napkin to the woman, he said, "That will be one thousand dollars."

The woman was stunned. "But that took you only a few seconds," she said.

"No, madam," Picasso replied, "that took me a lifetime."

The world has produced few visual literates the likes of Pablo Picasso. It takes natural talent and, as Picasso implied, a lifetime of struggle and suffering to reach such heights. Picasso dedicated his life to art. His work is hailed as some of the best ever produced by the human mind and hand. Picasso was one of a kind and he justly deserves his reputation. He certainly had an instinctive understanding of the power of dopamine and Your Three Second Window.

Few of us will ever reach such artistic greatness, but that doesn't mean you can't become a competent visual literate; in fact, to be successful in today's economy, you must! You can learn how to use the same visual concepts that Picasso and all other great artists used to create their masterpieces. Understanding the language of art—becoming a visual literate—gives you the power to exercise greater control over the impressions you make on others through the things you create. From the simplest written document to full-blown multimedia presentations, from a simple table setting for two to the design of a home, having command of the visual vocabulary will increase the joy and success you and those around you derive from everything you do and make. It's essential to getting the most out of the connections between aesthetics and the pleasure and decision-making centers of the brain and to mastering Your Three Second Window.

The principles presented here will not make you a great artist. What they will do is give you a basic understanding of the visual concepts that govern human perception. You'll be able to discern good design from bad design. You'll gain the power to create compositions that are pleasing to the eye, produce thoughts that are reasoned and elegant and develop communications that release the coveted shot of dopamine in your audience's brains. What you won't learn is how to produce "cutting-edge" work.

How often have you heard that phrase "cutting edge"? The term is applied to everything from advertising to automotive design. I'm sure you've been the victim of cutting-edge work in the form of multiple typefaces, busy backgrounds, garish colors and animated photos and film clips with jerky motion and bad sound. Often, the visually *illiterate* will try to breathe life into a poorly organized presentation by dressing it up with lots of gimmicks and calling it cutting edge. You can't really blame them. The advent of computer design programs such as PowerPoint has placed a great burden on people who have never had any training in visual literacy. It used to be that professional writers and designers produced communication pieces. Now everyone is expected to create his or her own, and most people are understandably lost. The state of art education in schools for the past few decades has been and continues to be woefully inadequate to equip most people to excel in the new economy.

A visual vocabulary is necessary to the creative process. A good idea will never see the light of day until it is given form. Today, visual literacy and creativity are important not only in the creation of visual and verbal communication, but in all aspects of life. There was a time when it was enough to be a linear thinker. A degree in accounting, law, engineering or business administration was enough to see a person through a life's career. But times have changed. I recently attended a book lecture by Dan Pink, author of *A Whole New Mind*, and he illustrated the situation better than I could ever hope to. Pink is a writer, a lawyer and a former speechwriter for Vice President Al Gore. Pink talks about what he calls the three A's as a way to describe the new world order as it applies to you and me.

Pink's first A stands for Asia, and he relates a few troubling facts:

- There are a billion people in India alone.

- Fifteen percent are highly educated in the professions and speak English fluently.

- Communication by phone and computer between India and the U.S. is virtually free.

- An Indian accountant makes about five hundred dollars a month.

You can see where this is going. Over a million Americans had their taxes done in India in 2007, and the number will no doubt go up. Much of the world's software engineering is being done in India. If you've ever had to deal with a big corporation's customer care department, you know where a lot of the call centers are now located, too. The jobs being performed in Asia are for the most part left-brain jobs—those tasks that require a linear style of thinking. Anything that can be accomplished by following a set of rules and instructions can be done more cheaply overseas than in America.

Pink's second A is for automation. Many of those same linear-thinking jobs now flowing to Asia are beginning to be done by computer programs. Computer programs are very good at following rules and instruction sets and can accomplish many tasks much more quickly and cheaply than even overseas professionals. An example Pink gives is the no-fault divorces now available on the Internet for a couple hundred dollars. What used to cost several thousand dollars in attorney's fees can now be accomplished in a few minutes at your keyboard. I recently saw no-fault divorces online for two hundred and forty-nine dollars.

The third A Pink talks about is aesthetics. Americans today are richer than any people who ever existed on Earth. If you took your great-great-grandparents to your home to see the wall-to-wall carpeted three thousand square feet of floor space, the microwave oven, the big-screen TV and the two new cars in the driveway, they'd think they had stumbled into King Farouk's summer home. And with affluence comes the ability to meet one's aesthetic needs. The American consumer is willing to pay a premium for good design. The example Pink gives is the case of the "aesthetically pleasing toilet brush." Pink ponders how, if he chose to enter the toilet brush market, he could position his product to compete in the marketplace of toilet brushes. He points out that toilet brush engineering has reached its apex; it's probably as good as it's ever going to be, so it would be very hard to compete on engineering. How about cost? With cheap overseas manufacturing, it would be virtually impossible to compete in the low-cost toilet brush market; they're probably being made about as cheaply as they ever will be. The only way Pink believes he could compete is through aesthetics. A toilet brush that was so beautifully designed it didn't have to be hidden beneath the sink would no doubt make a big splash (pun intended).

Pink comes to the conclusion that creativity is the new necessity for the American professional. To achieve success in today's economy of expanding world markets and increased competition, everyone needs not only linear-thinking abilities, but also the creativity to think and communicate in ways that are visually pleasing and compelling. To succeed in today's economy, you need to understand how to stimulate your own and others' reward systems in Your Three Second Window.

Learning to See

The first and most important step in unlocking your own creativity and applying it to your everyday life is learning to see as artists see. It's no secret that people are naturally curious and easily bored. They are more likely to sit up and pay attention to a new idea than they are to get excited about something they feel is familiar. Even an old idea presented in a new way will generate more interest than the same old thing presented the same old way. Artists are especially good at coming up with exciting, original ideas and at new ways of looking at old ideas to make them fresh and exciting to an audience. That's because when new connections are established in our brains as a result of understanding a new idea, we are rewarded with a pleasant feeling of accomplishment. The dopamine really gets flowing. One of the barriers to coming up with new ideas and presenting fresh perspectives on established ideas is the way we separate imagination from the real world.

We tend to think of the real world as something outside of ourselves and the world of our imagination as wholly within our minds. To understand how artists are able to introduce new ideas and create things that give us pleasing aesthetic experiences and stimulate our reward systems, we need to examine the relationship between the real world and imaginary world the way artists do. We need to adopt an artistic way of seeing.

In a way, both the real and imaginary worlds are simply pictures in our minds. To create a picture in the so-called real world, we collect information through our senses, which our brains use to create an image that we accept as real. For instance, our eyes might detect a certain combination of shapes, colors, lines and textures, which are then transmitted to the cerebral cortex, where those stimuli might be converted into an image of a tree. What that picture in our minds looks like has a lot to do with the quality of the light, the time of day, our proximity and a thousand other visual cues. That picture of the tree is also affected by what we expect to see; we all have a slightly different idea of what a tree should be, and that unconscious bias will influence how our brains interpret the visual data. All this data processing and converting of light rays into pictures of trees happens effortlessly, almost instantly and without our conscious knowledge.

To create a picture in the imaginary world takes a bit of conscious effort; we close our eyes, think of the same tree and bingo! The image of that tree reappears in our minds just as though we were actually seeing it in the real world. In a way, the real and imaginary worlds are the same, at least as far as our brains are concerned. This idea might seem a bit hard to swallow, but an example of the phenomenon is touched upon in the beginning of this book. Researchers who studied human brain activity using functional magnetic resonance imaging, which is capable of producing real-time images of brain function, found that the subjects' brain activity showed almost identical responses to the actual presence of loved ones and to photos of those same loved ones. As far as the brain's reward system is concerned, the image created in the brain by a photo was as real as the image created in the brain by the actual person.

In the real world, you can walk around a tree, look at it from different angles and at different distances. As you do, the picture of the tree in your brain changes. It gets bigger as you get closer, smaller as you get farther away. Shadows shift and textures become more or less evident. The wind blows and leaves shimmer in the sunlight. It becomes difficult to get an "accurate" and constant image of the tree because it won't stay still. The tree has many different characteristics that make up its constantly changing appearance. But the tree does have an essence—a reality separate from the way it looks. Jacques Riviere, the art critic, wrote: "The purpose of painting is to represent objects as they really are, that is to say different than the way we see them."

It's the artist's job to identify what it is about the tree that gives it its treeness. It could be the tree's strength or its height or perhaps its longevity. All these characteristics and more are valid subjects for the artist's efforts. When you look at a painting of the tree, you see something very different from what you perceive when viewing the tree in the real world. You are seeing what the artist sees. But both images are created in the very same way in the very same place in your brain.

Art, then, doesn't happen on the canvas but in our minds. Art breaks down the distinction between the real and imaginary worlds. It makes us think about the way we see and process information and gives us insight into how our minds work to make sense of our environment—and it's the way artists look at the world.

In art school, students are encouraged to challenge convention, discard fixed notions and explore different ways of seeing. Instead of looking at the world as having trees, houses, streets, rocks, mountains, streams and people, young artists are taught to see the environment not in terms of things, but in terms of shape, color, form, line, perspective, texture, shadow and myriad other visual elements. In other words, artists try to "de-objectify" the world and see it as if the brain had not converted all those light rays into "things." The famous artist Henri Matisse once said that "underlying this succession of moments which constitutes the superficial existence of things and beings, and which is continually modifying and transforming them, one can search for a truer, more essential character, which the artist will seize so that he may give to reality a more lasting interpretation."

The artist tries to create an image of the tree that goes beyond its mere appearance, to distill the essence of the tree and represent it in a way that expresses its truer nature. It's this different way of seeing that gives art its ability to create an emotional response, to make you think and to trigger your reward system to provide you with a pleasurable aesthetic experience.

Pablo Picasso supplies a dramatic example of how artists see differently to create works that transcend their subject matter. When Picasso first began to create his Cubist pictures, other painters were generally following the rules of perspective: Objects farther away were depicted as smaller, nearer objects were larger. These painters showed us the scene as though viewing it from a single point in space, as on a hill through a window or from some other specific place. Those paintings showed a scene frozen in time, a sort of snapshot of the world. Picasso, though, opened up a new way for us to see. He disregarded the classical rules followed by most painters of the time and replaced them with a more dynamic approach. Picasso wasn't so concerned about creating paintings that depicted an actual place as he was about creating paintings that show how we experience the world. He painted things in a more abstract manner, giving less importance to the way they appeared as static objects and focusing instead on the way we humans perceive them as we move through time and space. Like the tree that we see from different angles, different distances and in different light as we move around it in the real world, Picasso's paintings combined many different experiences into a single composition.

Instead of using conventional perspective, Picasso often placed all his objects on the same plane with conflicting light sources suggesting different viewing angles. People, rooms, bottles and musical instruments were abstracted to more geometric shapes, emphasizing their interconnectedness. The "imaginary" world Picasso created in his paintings depicted not only objects, but the passing of time as well. The result is that instead of being passive viewers, we become active participants in Picasso's Cubist paintings: We never see anything standing still, things are always changing, either we're rushing past them or they're rushing past us. In a way, Picasso's imaginary world is a lot like our real world.

Picasso's work broke with the past and invented a new way of seeing—a new way all his own. He got people thinking new thoughts, which is a very satisfying and pleasant thing to do. Showing people new ways of seeing is a very effective way of creating success. But it raises the question of *how* we see. It's helpful to understand how the brain processes visual information when we set out to get people excited about our own individual new ways of seeing and thinking. It's a powerful tool for creating Three Second Windows.

Seeing, from a neurological standpoint, is the result of a series of processes that occur almost instantly inside your brain. The process begins when light enters through your eyes and is transmitted to a part of your brain called the cerebral cortex, specifically a section called V1. V1 acts as a kind of router to distribute different kinds of visual information—such as color, shape, form and movement—to different sections of your cerebral cortex that are dedicated to processing those particular aspects of the visual world. These parallel systems of information processing are thought to have evolved to enable you to perceive and think more quickly and thus react faster to survival threats and opportunities. Recent studies also suggest that these systems can operate independently of each other and that they actually run at slightly different speeds. The result is that you tend to perceive, or "see," different aspects of the world before you see others. For instance, you tend to see color first, then form followed by motion. For example, you might first notice a flash of red in your rearview mirror, then recognize its form as that of a Ferrari and finally perceive that it is speeding up on your bumper.

Interestingly enough, the different parts of the cerebral cortex work by actually discarding certain kinds of information in order to extract only the information necessary to form a useful picture in your mind. In his essay "Art and the Brain," Semir Zeki elaborates on what kind of information is dispensed with by the cerebral cortex: "With colour, it is the precise wavelength composition of the light reflected from a surface that has to be discounted, whereas with size it is the precise viewing distance, and with form, the viewing angle."

Your brain is hardwired to be selective about what information gets included in seeing. It stores learned information, which it uses to reference new information and create the elements needed to form a mental picture. For instance, you might see a tree from a helicopter, a view you've never experienced before, but your brain is still able to compare this new visual stimulus with previous information and make the necessary adjustments to allow you to read the image as a tree.

The ability of the brain's visual system to be selective about what kind of information is included in our picture of the world gives a new meaning to the old saying "there's more to the world than meets the eye." It's tempting to speculate what the world would look like to us if our brains had evolved differently, or to think about the "invisible" parts of the world that we're just not equipped to perceive. In a way, that's just what artists do. They eliminate or play down some visual elements and emphasize others to create the emotional response desired. The brain, in its tendency to pull out or abstract only the meaningful information, performs a remarkably similar function.

In their essay "The Science of Art, A Neurological Theory of Aesthetic Experience," V.S. Ramachandran and William Hirstein discuss something neuro researchers call the Peak Shift Principle. To illustrate the Peak Shift Principle, they give the example of the baby seagull, whose brain is hardwired to cause it to peck at the mother's beak—which has a red dot on the end—to get food. In one study, researchers replaced the mother with a dummy beak sporting the same red dot and found that the chick pecked at the dummy beak the same way it pecked at a real one. Next, researchers put two red dots on the dummy beak and observed that the baby pecked even harder. In a third experiment, the beak was replaced with a stick that had three red stripes painted on it. The result? The baby seagull showed even greater enthusiasm than when presented with a dummy beak with two red dots. As the amount of redness increased, the degree of emotional response increased accordingly. By introducing a new idea—a stick with red stripes—based on a familiar concept—the mother seagull's beak with one red dot—the researchers were able to generate an increased level of interest and excitement.

Ramachandran and Hirstein make this interesting observation concerning the Peak Shift Principle: "If a rat is taught to discriminate a square from a rectangle and rewarded for the rectangle, it will soon learn to respond more frequently to the rectangle. Paradoxically, however, the rat's response to a rectangle that is even longer and skinnier is even greater than it was to the original prototype on which it was trained. This curious result implies that what the rat is learning is not a prototype but a rule, i.e., *rectangularity*."

They suggest that the Peak Shift Principle is exhibited in the behavior of humans, too: "What the artist tries to do (either consciously or subconsciously) is to not only capture the essence of something but also to amplify it in order to more powerfully activate the same neural mechanisms that would be activated by the original object."

When Picasso made his great breakthrough in painting, his new ideas about seeing were based solidly in, and grew out of, his and other artists' previous work. His painting was also influenced by ideas from other contemporary thinkers. It's no surprise that Picasso's time was one of great revolutions not only in painting, but in math and physics, too. In the early twentieth century, about the same time Picasso was inventing Cubism, Albert Einstein was publishing his paper on the special theory of relativity. Einstein challenged old, Newtonian ways of thinking about time and space, proposing that they are not in fact separate as our intuition tells us, but one and the same: the time-space continuum.

In his book *Smart World*, Richard Ogle talks about this very idea: "It was part of Picasso's genius to have intuitively recognized very early the significance of this historic scientific shift. Furthermore, once the basic move to abstraction had been made, much followed almost automatically. Abstract form, like mathematics itself, proved to be a rich generative engine....Picasso and Braque, influenced by radical new theories in mathematics and physics that destroyed the unity of a single perspective, discovered this for themselves, and then created an art that allowed the viewer to discover it too."

We can imagine the pleasure that Picasso's paintings created (and still do create) in those viewers who participated in his experimental way of seeing. The feelings of wonder, discovery and satisfaction that come from figuring out and understanding a new idea have few equals in the range of human enjoyment.

The Divine Proportion

The ancients understood the value of creativity. It was so important in times past that the greatest minds of history were turned toward figuring out how to make things beautiful. Over the centuries, artists, philosophers and scientists such as Da Vinci, Bruneschelli and Le Corbusier struggled to find ways to capture creativity in a formula, equation or set of rules. The result is the body of aesthetic knowledge we have today. Unfortunately, due to a scandalous lack of artistic training in primary and secondary education, the art and craft of creating aesthetically pleasing experiences have become, in modern times, mostly the bailiwick of trained designers and artists. But it doesn't have to be that way. Visual literacy is not beyond the reach of practically every person on Earth. We all respond to pleasurable aesthetics, so why shouldn't we be able to create them, too? All we need is to understand the principles and to practice them a bit. There's only one Picasso, but with a little effort, you can achieve a level of visual literacy to create Three Second Windows that inspire and motivate others and help you succeed.

One of the earliest things artists took note of was that some shapes and proportions are more pleasing to the senses than others. It was also observed that these shapes and proportions worked all across the spectrum of human endeavor. Architecture, painting, music and, later, interior design, typography, photography and graphic design could equally benefit from the same certain set of relationships. This set of proportions could be scaled from the size of a postage stamp to an entire city and still work beautifully. There is much speculation about just why these relationships stimulate our reward systems and provide that shot of dopamine that tells us our human needs are being met, but there is universal agreement that they do. Many proportions stimulate the reward system to produce dopamine. Some are specific to the human and animal form, while others are more suited to small-scale things such as sheets of paper, books and magazines. Still others reveal themselves in grander ways: the great pyramids, the Parthenon, Notre Dame. But there is one set of proportions that seems to trump them all, a set of proportions that encompasses all aspects of life, from nature to man-made objects, from the smallest DNA molecule to the greatest feats of architecture. I'm talking about the golden ratio, first mentioned by Euclid (325–265 B.C.), who defined it as *the division of a line in extreme and mean ratio.* Later, in a volume illustrated by Leonardo Da Vinci, Luca Pacioli (1445–1517) wrote about the golden ratio in his treatise *De Divina Proportione.* Even before the golden ratio was described, it seems humans were employing it instinctively. Buildings from the time of ancient Egypt to the present can be analyzed through the use of the golden ratio. Approximations of the golden ratio are evident in the Giza pyramids and even Mesoamerican architecture.

The golden ratio is such a powerful aesthetic tool that it's worth looking at closely and discussing at length. Here's how it works: The golden ratio is a line unevenly divided in two, so that the shorter section has the same ratio to the longer section as the longer section has to the whole line and vice versa. In other words, the big has a resemblance to the small. The golden ratio can be used to create many different geometric shapes, including spirals, rectangles, pentagrams and stars, to name but a few. Mathematically, an example of the golden ratio can be represented like this:

1 is to 3 as 3 is to 9

with three being the golden mean, or the number that binds the other two numbers together in a natural kind of unity and harmony. The golden ratio is expressed in nature through the Fibonacci Sequence—which if you are among the millions who read *The Da Vinci Code* will be immediately familiar to you as a series of numbers in which each number is the sum of the preceding two numbers:

0, 1, 1, 2, 3, 5, 8, 13, 21, 34, 55, 89, 144, 233, 377 and so on

Fibonacci Sequence golden ratios are found in nature and are routinely used by designers and architects to construct aesthetically pleasing compositions. There is a mysterious connection between the golden ratio and life. It seems to pop up everywhere and serve as a unifying force in the organization of all living things. For instance, the arrangement of leaves on many plants reveals the golden ratio, an organization of angles that just happens to provide for the most efficient photosynthesis, water delivery to roots and insect pollination. The pussy willow grows in a pattern that conforms to the Fibonacci golden ratio with five spirals and thirteen buds. The shell of a turtle has thirteen horn plates, five in the center and eight along the edges. Our own bodies reveal the presence of the Fibonacci golden ratio: The three bones of each of your fingers are the golden ratio and if you were to measure the distance from your navel to the top of your head, you'd discover a close approximation of the golden ratio. The Fibonacci golden ratio even shows up in your self-organizing DNA nucleotides.

The golden ratio has been the inspiration behind the design of countless great buildings, including the Parthenon, Notre Dame Cathedral and the United Nations building. It seems that the golden ratio is everywhere we look. But why does it hold such appeal for us? Why does it stimulate our reward systems? Why is it such a good structure for organizing information? Some who have made a study of the golden ratio believe its power lies in the very fact that it seems woven into so much of the fabric of life, connecting humans to nature and each other in a harmonious way.

Mario Livio, in his book *The Golden Ratio: The Story of Phi, the World's Most Astonishing Number,* writes:

> Some of the greatest mathematical minds of all ages, from Pythagoras and Euclid in ancient Greece, through the medieval Italian mathematician Leonardo of Pisa and the Renaissance astronomer, Johannes Kepler, to present-day scientific figures such as Oxford physicist Roger Penrose, have spent endless hours over this simple ratio and its properties. But the fascination with the golden ratio is not confined just to mathematicians. Biologists, artists, musicians, historians, architects, psychologists, and even mystics have pondered and debated the basis of its ubiquity and appeal. In fact, it is probably fair to say that the golden ratio has inspired thinkers of all disciplines like no other number in the history of mathematics.

Sound enticing? You can use the golden ratio to create your own golden rectangles. When you are creating a composition, whether on paper, on a screen or even in the arrangement of furniture, you can use the golden ratio to create countless shapes and relationships that will provide aesthetic pleasure and a sense of unity and harmony. Follow the simple instructions included here to see if you like the golden section more than other shapes. Take a few moments to observe what's around you and see if you can spot the golden section in buildings, automobiles, billboards, magazines and books. Pay close attention to the proportions of houses and their doors and windows. You don't need to carry a tape measure with you. Just look closely and soon you'll be able to identify the golden section with just a glance. As you take part in this exercise, notice whether some shapes are more pleasing to the eye than others. Do you feel that some are "right," while others leave you feeling a bit uneasy? After a short time you'll become adept at spotting the golden section everywhere you go. Pay attention to the way it makes you feel. Is your reward system giving you that little shot of dopamine? If you're like most of us, the answer will probably be yes.

In fact, there is scientific evidence to suggest that we humans do respond positively to the golden section. A study conducted at the Department of Neuroscience at the University of Parma, Italy used fMRI brain scanning to show that subjects preferred the classical canonical proportions of the golden ratio (1:1.618) over others. Subjects were shown images of the classical sculpture, Doryphoros by Polykletos in its original proportion, and asked to rate its beauty in comparison with images of the same sculpture, only with the proportions modified to make the legs shorter or the trunk longer. Researchers watched how the brain functioned and discovered that those regions having to do with emotions were more active, which suggest that the images revealing the golden section activated the subjects' reward systems to a greater degree than the non-golden-section images. It turns out, viewing the golden section actually made people *feel* better!

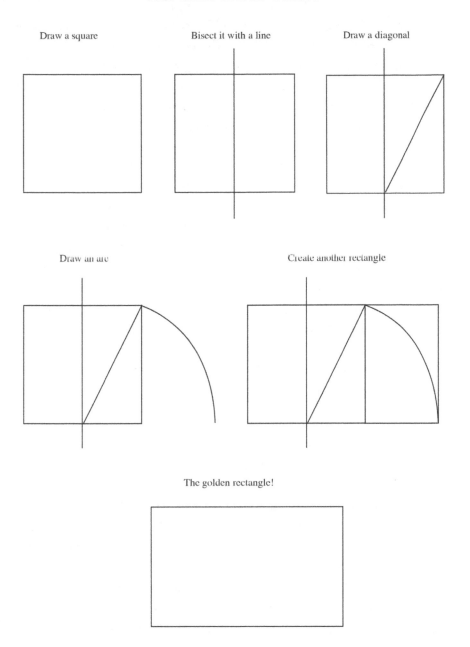

Draw a square — Bisect it with a line — Draw a diagonal

Draw an arc — Create another rectangle

The golden rectangle!

Composition

The golden section can be used as a basis for all kinds of compositions. It can be used as a guide when sizing photographs or drawings. It can be used to create the margins of a presentation. You can divide your living room and wall space in pleasing ways using the golden section. A dinner place setting could be based on the golden section. The possibilities are limited only by your imagination. The golden section is an interesting phenomenon, but for it to be useful, you have to understand how to construct shapes that bring aesthetic pleasure and unity. You have to understand how composition—the foundation of all visual communication—works.

Composition is simply the arrangement of elements in a space. Whether it's a painting, a business document, a room, a building or an entire landscape, deciding how the different parts are going relate to each other is the first and most important step toward creating a successful composition. Trying to create a pleasing composition without having some concrete starting point can be very frustrating. Where does this picture go? What about this type? As you change one element, it affects the placement of another. Without a solid understanding and grounding in the principles of composition, the outcome is probably going to be the product of chance. You might get lucky once in a while and come up with something pleasing by accident, but leaving the effectiveness of your efforts to happenstance is risky business indeed. It's no way to create compelling Three Second Windows.

There's a lot that goes into the creation of a pleasing composition, but success will elude you unless you understand one basic concept first: positive and negative space. Once you have a grasp of this basic concept, the rest will fall into place.

When I was a young graduate student at the Rhode Island School of Design, I had a summer job teaching design classes to gifted high school students from all over the U.S. and the world. Most of the aspiring designers would come to class the first day expecting to dive right into making rock band posters or fashion magazine layouts. Imagine their disappointment when they received their first assignment: to arrange black and white squares on a ten-inch by ten-inch board. "What's this got to do with design?" they'd complain.

"Ask me that in six weeks," I'd reply.

The object of this first assignment was to give students the power to control their compositions through the manipulation of positive and negative space, also known as figure and ground. To the untrained eye, an image on a page is just that. But to the visual literate, it's much more. Have you ever wondered why some things you see seem just right, while others are a little, or a lot, off? You might be flipping through a magazine or surfing the Web when you come across a page that is so pleasing to the eye you just have to stop and gaze at it a bit longer. You feel the little release of dopamine and you have a pleasant Three Second Window. The reverse is true, too. Sometimes you'll see a page that is so ugly you can't hurry past it fast enough. What is it that makes some things naturally pleasing and others objectionable? A lot goes into the equation, but you can bet your bottom dollar that composition is at the heart of it.

Good design starts with good composition. Without it, the result will be bad no matter what. So what is good composition? Simply put, it is a harmonious relationship between positive and negative space. When there is interconnectedness between things, harmony—and its accompanying shot of dopamine—results. To create that harmonious relationship, you have to be able to "see" the negative space. Positive space is pretty easy to recognize, because it's made up of the objects placed on the page. Positive space might be photographs, drawings, shapes, blocks of color, type or just about anything you can think of that has a visual presence. And that's where the difficulty lies. We tend to think of those objects as the only important elements in a composition. We tend to think of the white, or negative space, they create as left over and not important. Many novices are bothered by this "left over" space and try to fill it up, usually resulting in a cluttered and clumsy composition. What they are responding to is the lack of harmony between the positive and negative space. The truth is, the left-over, or negative, space makes as big a contribution to composition as do the objects, or positive space. Understanding and accepting this basic truth is crucial to being able to see and use negative space in visually pleasing ways.

Negative space has a visual presence that is just as important to our subconscious brains as positive space. To recognize negative space, we need to retrain our conscious brains to see in a different way. We need to learn to elevate that subconscious knowledge to a plane of awareness. In other words, we need to learn to see as artists. This might sound like a daunting task and at first it can be. My gifted high school students would sometimes struggle with the idea of negative space for days, but eventually, one by one, the lights would go on. I could tell the instant students "saw" negative space. Their eyes would light up, their jaws would drop, quickly followed by a broad grin. It was a life-changing Three Second Window. It was the moment they became visual literates.

Once students learned to control the negative space and incorporate it into a composition, they were able to create things that had vibrancy and life that were lacking in their work before. Sometimes a student would create a pleasing composition without understanding the concept of positive and negative space, but these happy accidents were rarities.

Students were assigned the task of creating an aesthetically pleasing composition using only black and white squares. Part of the assignment was to have equal amounts of positive and negative space. Notice how the white squares (negative space) are as easy to see as the black squares (positive space). This is called "activating the negative space" or "integrating figure and ground."

While positive and negative space form the basics of composition, there are different ways of using positive and negative space to express your message effectively. Generally speaking, composition can be divided into two types: static and dynamic. Static composition communicates calm, quiet and a state of rest. Dynamic composition conveys motion, activity and verve. Each type has its place, so it's important to understand the difference.

The difference between static and dynamic composition is not easy to describe in words, but in general terms, it could be said that while static composition is often symmetrical, dynamic composition is just as often asymmetrical, although this isn't always the case. In the hands of a competent designer, both static and dynamic composition can be symmetrical or asymmetrical, or in some cases both!

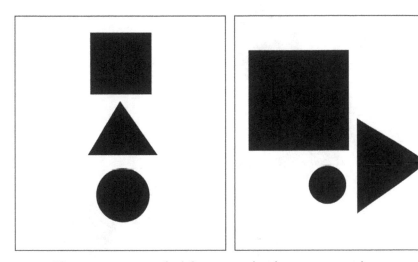

The composition on the left is static; the objects appear to be at rest.
The composition on the right is dynamic; the relationship between
the objects is less predictable, there is a greater variety of scale and the
negative space is more varied and active. Creating pleasing compositions
depends on the ability to manipulate and activate negative space.

As you learn to control composition through the manipulation of positive and negative space, you'll find it useful to employ certain other visual concepts that will help you create the exact look you want. Harmony, rhythm, emphasis, tension, proportion, symmetry and unity are visual concepts integral to an aesthetically pleasing composition, the release of dopamine by the reward system and the creation of a powerful Three Second Window.

Harmony

A harmonious relationship exists between elements when they share certain colors or shapes or a progression in size, shape or other characteristics that binds them together in ways that are pleasing to the eye.

Harmony is created between the different shapes
through the use of alignment and angle.

Rhythm

Just as rhythm can produce an aesthetically pleasing experience in music, so can it stimulate the senses in a positive way through visual communication. Visual rhythm can be defined as a harmonious relationship between *the change* in elements such as images and type and between positive and negative space. Visual rhythm can also help tell your story by suggesting movement in one or more directions, a sequence of events or ideas and unity of thought. Through visual rhythm, elements on the page or screen can lead the eye from one place to another, even from one page or screen to another. When arranging elements on a page or screen to create visual rhythm, it's important to relate them to each other through shape, scale, alignment and spacing. One or more common elements can be used to tie the composition together in an aesthetically pleasing way.

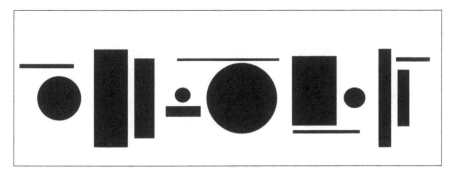

Visual rhythm adds life and energy to any composition.

Emphasis

Emphasis is the focusing of attention on one or more particular points in the composition. Emphasis can be created through the use of color, shape, position or any number of other visual tactics.

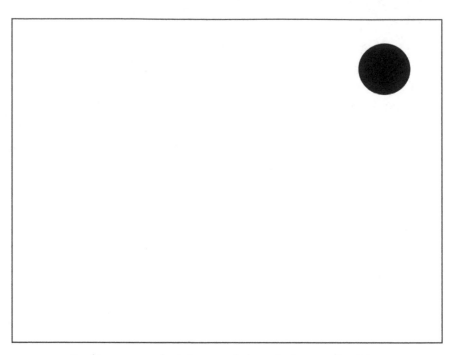

In this case, emphasis is created through the use of position.

Tension

When we think of tension, we usually think of emotional stress or something a bit more literal, such as a tightly wound guitar string. But when we talk about tension in design, we're talking about something else entirely: visual tension, and I don't mean the kind that comes from reading this book in low light. Visual tension is a concept in art and design that refers to the imaginary stress that exists between two elements in close relationship to each other. The eye is good at measuring distances between things, and the subconscious brain is good at assigning a value of sorts to those relationships. Things that are very close together produce a sense of high tension. As they approach each other, the tension increases until they actually meet, when the tension disappears. It's almost like watching two cars about to crash. The excitement and concern reach their peak just before impact; once the impact occurs, the outcome is known and the sense of tension lessens. You can use visual tension to draw the eye to an important image, to create a sense of excitement or to highlight some key information.

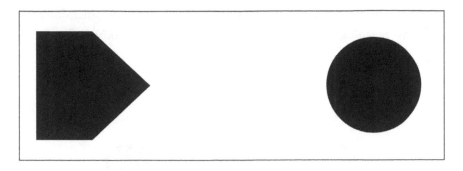

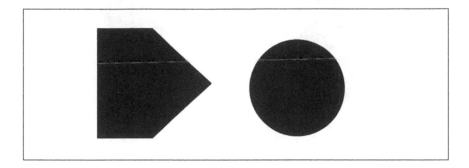

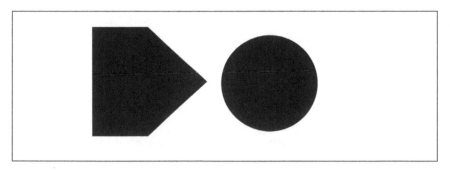

Notice how the visual tension increases as the shapes get closer together. Tension is greatest at the point where the triangle almost touches the circle, and the negative space becomes more activated and energized.

Proportion

Proportion is the relative size between elements and can apply to both positive and negative space. Proportion can be used to create the illusion of depth in two dimensions, attract the eye to important points, create visual hierarchy and draw meaningful comparisons between different and similar elements.

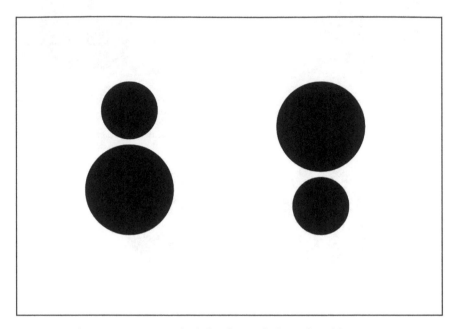

The composition on the left is better balanced and has a more pleasing proportional relationship than the one on the right.

Symmetry

When we think of symmetry, we usually think of things being evenly balanced. In the world of visual literacy, however, there are actually many kinds of symmetry. Asymmetry is a kind of symmetry, for instance, that creates unequal balance. Symmetry and asymmetry can be used to create an overall feeling of calm or action.

Symmetrical balance.

Asymmetrical balance.
The negative space balances out the positive space in a pleasing way.

Unity

When we look up at the nighttime sky and trace the constellations, we are creating relationships between stars that exist only in our imaginations. We see bears, archers, rams and many other familiar shapes. The brain's natural inclination to form groups out of different objects accounts for this phenomenon. The subconscious is always looking for order in the world, whether it is actually there or not. You can use the brain's desire for order to help communicate your message. Creating a sense of unity helps your audience follow your story and makes communication quicker and easier to understand. Through unity, you can make a visual connection between certain important related ideas and also separate different thoughts from each other. We tend to group different objects by different criteria, such as shape, position, color or proximity.

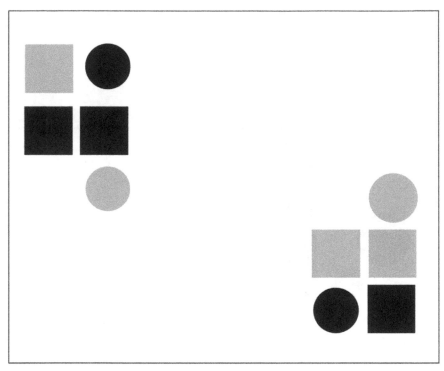

The subconscious brain tends to look for and create order. It will group objects together using shape, position, color and proximity as criteria.

Craft

We already know how attuned the brain is to detail. The smallest defect in execution is picked up by the subconscious and can spoil even the most carefully created Three Second Window. And although the conscious brain doesn't always notice such things right away, they can manifest as a nagging sense that something isn't quite right. It could be as simple as an ink smudge or as glaring as a photo placed upside down. I remember when one of my design professors, a person of international fame, showed me a mistake in a book on his life. There was a photo of him and his family, with his children and wife identified in the caption. The only problem was that one of the young men in the photo was not his son, but rather a graduate student who just happened to appear in the photo. The professor was delighted at the error and thought it was a subject of great hilarity. I asked him how he could have let the author get away with such an obvious mistake. "I was busy with something else that day," he said with a shrug and a smile. "I just didn't look closely enough."

Craft is as important to a communication as any other thing that goes into creating a compelling message. Everything you do must be clearly intentional. Even if you are trying to express randomness, you'll have to work hard to make it clear that is the meaning. It's inevitable that we will make mistakes in the initial stages. There will be typos, photos will be in the wrong place or slightly out of line, borders will be uneven. That's why it's so important to have fresh eyes go over your work from time to time and certainly you want second and third persons to proofread and point out errors or questionable design decisions before your audience ever catches a glimpse.

Color

The visual literate controls the effect of color the same way he or she controls composition. One of the most important things to know about color is how to talk about it. Most of us know the primary colors of red, blue and yellow. Many understand the secondary colors that are mixtures of the primary colors: Red and blue make purple, red and yellow make orange, blue and yellow make green. A few know about the tertiary colors, which are produced when a primary color is mixed with a secondary color; examples are yellow-orange, red-orange, red-violet, blue-violet, blue-green and yellow-green. When we think about color, it's important to use the right words.

- *Hue* is the name of a color, such as red or purple.

- *Tint* is the addition of white to any hue.

- *Shade* is the addition of black to any hue.

- *Contrast* is the difference in intensity and hue between hues.

- *Intensity* is the brightness of a hue.

- *Saturation* is the visual depth of a hue.

The Bauhaus artist Joseph Albers spent a lifetime experimenting with color. In his seminal book on the subject, *The Interaction of Color*, Albers shows how the perception of a color depends upon its relationship to the colors around it. Green can be made to look like a shade of blue, and purple can be made to look very reddish in one context and to have a bluish cast in another. In some of Albers' studies, amazing changes occur to the same color when the colors around it change. The lesson to learn is that color is the most relative of the design elements you are likely to be dealing with. It's not so important what individual color you choose, as the *set* of colors you choose. Think of your colors as the actors in a play. There will be your lead character along with a supporting cast that will interact with the star of the show. Choose a main color, then put other colors beside and around it. Compare the feeling you get by isolating each of the properties as they relate to the main color: hue, tint, shade, contrast, intensity, and saturation. Give each relationship the dopamine test and pick the winners. You'll come up with a color palette that will add punch and style to your communication every time.

Proportional Systems

The golden ratio is only one of many proportional systems that can be used to create rhythm, harmony and unity in Your Three Second Window. Graphic designers often use grids based on the golden ratio as well as squares, double squares and other building blocks to organize type and images on a page and to provide continuity with other parts of the communication. Grids are especially useful when working with multiple pages or screens, because they lend a consistent positional and proportional relationship throughout without sacrificing visual variety. Grids and other proportional systems accomplish their tasks through the employment of structure, parts and program. Think of the grid as a system with interacting elements that produce a certain overall visual effect. Each page or screen shows a cohesiveness that in turn relates to other pages or screens. Let's take a closer look each element.

Structure is that part of the grid that determines the *possible* placement of parts such as type and images. Photos and other images, headlines and subheads line up with the coordinates of the grid to provide a sense of order. Image size and proportion are constrained by the limitations of the grid coordinates.

Parts are elements that will take up space within the grid system, such as blocks of type, photos or illustrations and charts and graphs (and of course, negative space).

Program is that element of the grid system that determines where the parts can be and what size and proportion they can assume. Headlines and subheads can be confined to a certain position, say, at the upper left corner. Program can also determine the size of the headlines and subheads and the color. You might want to place an image in a certain repeating position within the grid on each page or screen or use blocks of color or rules to give your communication a livelier feel. An important function of the gird that should not be overlooked is its ability to help you create a hierarchy of information. For instance, you might want to place the key thought at a certain grid coordinate, then line up your support points in relationship to that key point in a way that makes it clear they are of secondary importance. Repeating this alignment for each key thought and group of support points on each page or slide makes it easier for your audience to understand what you are trying to say.

A note of caution when using proportional systems such as grids: While a grid can be of immense help in creating compelling and orderly communication, slavish observance to its restrictions can produce an overly predictable and boring composition. It's important to use your imagination and look for interesting and fresh ways to use the grid. And remember, it's a tool, and you are its master, not the other way around. It's okay, in fact desirable, to "break" the grid now and then to provide an occasional breather for the eye. Run an image past the grid coordinates, use an outlined photo or illustration, let it break free of its box now and then and run wild.

Designers often use grids like this one to organize information
on a page. This grid is based on the golden rectangle. The page
is a golden rectangle, as are the rectangles inside it.

 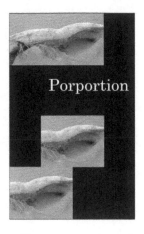 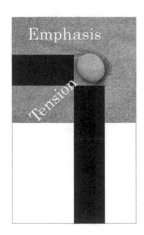

An example of three different compositions based on the same grid.
Notice the sense of variety created while still maintaining unity.

There's a lot to know about creating aesthetically pleasing experiences, and most professional designers and artists spend their lives in the pursuit of unattainable perfection. Alas, no perfect communication ever existed nor is it likely that one ever will. It's said that art is never finished, it's simply abandoned. A corollary to that old saw is "perfect is the enemy of good." Understanding the simple lessons in this chapter will give you the vocabulary and the eye to stimulate your own and others' reward systems, trigger the release of dopamine and make the most of every Three Second Window. Learning the principles of good design and practicing them in everything you do will help you produce strong, aesthetically pleasing communications that will help you succeed.

Chapter 10

The Holistic Effect

Chances are, your life is complex and varied, presenting scores—even hundreds—of different Three Second Windows every day. Some are small, others big; in the end, it's the cumulative effect of your decisions that adds up to success or failure. The more everyday moments you change into extraordinary opportunities, the more successful you'll be.

We're all unique and there's no one road to success that will work for everyone. You have to create your own. The Tao saying "The path that can be named is not the true path" contains much wisdom. I have always taken it to mean that we have to blaze our own trails in life. The exact approach that has worked for me won't necessarily work for you. That's why, in this book, I've avoided describing a neat and tidy way for you to be successful in all the spheres of your life. Instead, I've tried to give you the tools you need to help you create your own approach or system. But to create your own path, you need to understand a bit about what systems are and how they work.

A Short Course on Systems

Have you ever taken a close look at a piece of braided rope and wondered why there are several strands twisted together? At first thought, it would seem simpler to make one big strand instead of going to all the trouble of manufacturing three or four or five strands, then twisting them together. The truth is, that twisted rope is much stronger than a single strand of the same diameter would be. Why? Because of something called the holistic effect.

The holistic effect is based on an idea we've all heard stated: "The whole is greater than the sum of its parts." The holistic effect works like this: Say each individual strand of the rope can hold one hundred pounds of weight. If we were to construct a rope of three such strands untwisted, side by side, the total weight-bearing capacity of the rope would be a simple sum of the strength of each strand, or three hundred pounds. But if we twist those same three strands together, something marvelous happens. Now the weight-bearing capacity is greater than the simple sum of each strand. The rope *system* can hold more than three hundred pounds. The difference in strength between the strands untwisted and twisted is the holistic effect.

The production of a holistic effect is the difference between a collection of parts and a system. The rope untwisted is not a system because no holistic effect is produced. The rope twisted is a system because a holistic effect *is* produced. The better the system, the greater the holistic effect that comes out of it.

Now, you might be asking yourself, "What has a rope got to do with creating success in my life?"

The answer is, a lot.

As we've seen above, the definition of a system goes something like this: "A set of parts working together to create some holistic effect." The set of parts could be made up of furniture and walls, shirts and pants, words and pictures, positive and negative space, body language or just about anything you can think of. Your home is a system that produces the holistic effects of warmth and shelter. Your wardrobe is a system that produces the holistic effects of comfort and image. Every document you produce is a system that creates the holistic effects of entertainment, information and persuasion in others. *You* are a system capable of producing the holistic effect of success in everything you do, say, make and wear.

Your very life at this moment is a system. You rise in the morning, eat, dress, travel to your place of work. You interact with other people, other systems. They become a part of your system and you a part of theirs. Creating systems for creating success sounds, I admit, a bit academic, but it's a lot easier than it sounds, and it's extremely practical. In fact, you're already doing it! All you have to do to be more successful at it is make a slight change in the way you think by looking at the world as a system of systems. Everything around you is a system and also part of a bigger system, a smaller system and other, parallel systems, all at the same time. The trick lies in being able to pick out those individual systems, mix and match them in your mind and use them to create success in your life.

This theory of systems has applications everywhere. It works in all kinds of ways—in nature, in things people build and in ideas. The idea of successful living is not a new one. It has been around since the dawn of time. What is new is looking at success as a system: ideas, strategies and tactics that when used together allow you to accomplish a lot more than you could using any one or two of them alone.

When Systems Collide

Perhaps the system we are all most familiar with is our wardrobe. The clothes we choose to wear each day produce many holistic effects. If it's cold, we wear a sweater to produce the holistic effect of comfort. If we have an important meeting, we wear our finest to produce the holistic effect of a positive image. Usually we create a clothing system that is flexible, has interchangeable parts and works well to produce the effects we want. But there are those times when we get it wrong and the holistic effect is not the one we intended. It works with our clothes, and it works with our lives, too.

Back in 1983, the first day of classes for the new semester at the Rhode Island School of Design (RISD) proved to be a real cultural shock for me. Fresh from then provincial Seattle, I showed up attired in my regular West Coast garb: polo shirt, khaki pants and penny loafers. That morning I found myself standing in line next to a young man dressed completely in black who was wearing white face makeup and had a sixteen-inch-tall mohawk hairdo. And *I* was the one who stood out. We were, after all, at *Art School*. And not just any art school. Members of the conceptual music group Talking Heads had all been students there, and their breakthrough single, "Burning Down the

House," was topping the charts all over the country. RISD was the center of the avant-garde, and the students were making sure everyone knew it by the way they dressed. As I looked around, I noticed the other students nudging their friends and shooting me sly glances. I felt very out of place and, yes, a little stupid. My clothing didn't fit with the RISD clothing system.

I was dressed the way I usually dressed, in the way that made me feel comfortable. My clothes were producing a holistic effect all right; it was just the wrong holistic effect. Compared to the other RISD people, I was the square from the hinterland and ten years behind the fashion curve.

Even though I hadn't seen myself as a bumpkin when I got dressed that morning, I sure felt that way as I stood alone in a sea of art school hipness, sporting my earth-toned preppy Izod. The clothing system I had created that morning meshed perfectly with the Seattle clothing system I knew well, but in the context of the RISD clothing system, it was throwing a monkey wrench in the gears.

The next day, I showed up for the first day of class wearing the same Seattle outfit, dreading it a little, but when I got settled in my graduate studio and started meeting the other graphic designers, I breathed a sigh of relief. There was a student from Holland who came wearing a scarf, one from Chicago in a spiffy sport coat, another from New York City dressed in punk and ragged jeans and one fellow from Montana clad in denim and cowboy boots. Although we were all dressed differently, our eclectic look served to bind us together and over the next two years, we blended our wardrobes to create a kind of "RISD Grad Student Look," which was just catching on as I finished up my studies and moved on.

A successful life is a holistic effect of a carefully constructed system. Each part will interact with other parts, so it's important to consider each one and think about how its inclusion, omission or substitution will impact the holistic effect. To get the most out of "system thinking," you need to learn a slightly new way of thinking, to retrain your brain to see in original and interesting ways. It's not difficult—it's something artists learn to do early in their educations and they practice it every day.

In the preceding chapters, we explored the concepts that I've found work well together to create success in all phases of life. I'm sure you'll find some of the ideas more useful than others, and the beauty is that you'll be able to find new and unique ways of combining these ideas into your own systems and to develop your own way of creating success in everything you do and make. Just as the rope is made stronger by weaving together its strands, you too can weave together the ideas in this book to be more successful in all aspects of your life.

The real power in thinking of the world in terms of systems is that we begin to see that not only are we systems ourselves, we are also all part of many other systems. We're part of our family system, our friends system, our community system, our transportation system...well, you get the idea. There are a lot of systems and they all, in one way or another, at one time or another, interconnect and overlap. Understanding how we connect with others through the various systems available to us gives us a new ability to create our own unique systems of living that provide us the power to change everyday moments into new opportunities for success and make the most out of each and every Three Second Window.

This book is not the end all and be all. It's only a starting point meant to give you new ideas and to stimulate new ways of thinking, doing and being. Simply reading this book will do nothing to help you turn your everyday moments into new opportunities for success. You have to act to employ the principles presented, to practice them and make them your own. You must weave together the ideas and create powerful Three Second Windows every day.

It's up to you!

Get your free download

How to Avoid Death by PowerPoint®

Learn the seven simple steps to a perfect presentation.

This popular seminar usually costs **$249** but it's **FREE** when you log onto www.darbyroachpowerpoint.com.

You'll learn how to quickly create effective PowerPoint presentations using these seven principles of design:

- Strategy
- The Power of Three
- Composition
- Type
- Typography
- Color
- Image

EXTRA BONUS

As an added bonus, you'll get the complete set of Designer's PowerPoint Grids to help you create dynamic presentations that will rivet your audience and get your point across with impact and style!

Visit **www.darbyroachpowerpoint.com** today for your FREE guide to the perfect PowerPoint presentation!

About the Author

Teacher, writer, designer and businessman, Darby Roach has spent the last 25 years helping students and clients get the most out of their own Three Second Windows. In addition, Darby has used the principles presented in Your Three Second Window to create powerful marketing communications for marquee companies such as:

- Apple Computer
- Nike
- Microsoft
- T-Mobile
- Westin Hotels and Resorts
- HP
- Plus many others

Darby lives and works in Seattle, Washington. To find out more about Darby visit www.darbyroach.com. To find out about Darby's marketing agency, Orbit Direct, visit www.orbitdcm.com.

Chapter End Notes

Chapter 1

1 Steven Gangestad and Randy Thornhill 1990

2 Helen Fisher 2004

3 Jeremy N. Bailenson, Shanto Iyengar and Nick Yee 2004

4 Malia Mason 2005

5 Carlin Flora 2005

Chapter 2

1 Harp, Stretch, and Harp, 1985

Chapter 3

1 AP Dijksterhuis, W. Bos, Loran F. Nordgren, Rick B. van Barren

BUY A SHARE OF THE FUTURE IN YOUR COMMUNITY

These certificates make great holiday, graduation and birthday gifts that can be personalized with the recipient's name. The cost of one S.H.A.R.E. or one square foot is $54.17. The personalized certificate is suitable for framing and will state the number of shares purchased and the amount of each share, as well as the recipient's name. The home that you participate in "building" will last for many years and will continue to grow in value.

Here is a sample SHARE certificate:

THIS CERTIFIES THAT

YOUR NAME HERE

HAS INVESTED IN A HOME FOR A DESERVING FAMILY

1985-2005

TWENTY YEARS OF BUILDING FUTURES IN OUR COMMUNITY ONE HOME AT A TIME

1200 SQUARE FOOT HOUSE @ $65,000 = $54.17 PER SQUARE FOOT
This certificate represents a tax deductible donation. It has no cash value.

YES, I WOULD LIKE TO HELP!

I support the work that Habitat for Humanity does and I want to be part of the excitement! As a donor, I will receive periodic updates on your construction activities but, more importantly, I know my gift will help a family in our community realize the dream of homeownership. **I would like to SHARE in your efforts against substandard housing in my community!** *(Please print below)*

PLEASE SEND ME _____ SHARES at $54.17 EACH = $ $_____

In Honor Of: _____

Occasion: (Circle One)   HOLIDAY   BIRTHDAY   ANNIVERSARY

OTHER: _____

Address of Recipient: _____

Gift From: _____ *Donor Address:* _____

Donor Email: _____

I AM ENCLOSING A CHECK FOR $ $_____ PAYABLE TO HABITAT FOR HUMANITY OR PLEASE CHARGE MY VISA OR MASTERCARD *(CIRCLE ONE)*

Card Number _____ Expiration Date: _____

Name as it appears on Credit Card _____ Charge Amount $ _____

Signature _____

Billing Address _____

Telephone # Day _____ Eve _____

PLEASE NOTE: Your contribution is tax-deductible to the fullest extent allowed by law.
Habitat for Humanity • P.O. Box 1443 • Newport News, VA 23601 • 757-596-5553
www.HelpHabitatforHumanity.org

Printed in the USA
CPSIA information can be obtained
at www.ICGtesting.com
JSHW082200140824
68134JS00014B/349